ICEFALL

ISBN: 0692594140
ISBN-13: 978-0692594148

*For Granddad, Pasang Temba, Kumar Rai
and Tenzing Bhote*

CONTENTS

Part 1: Adversity 1

Part 2: Discovery 25

Part 3: Long & Winding Road 56

Part 4: False Horizon 104

Part 5: Resilience 141

Part 6: Avalanche 195

Epilogue 249

Acknowledgements 250

Index 255

PART 1

ADVERSITY

CHAPTER 1

Foothills

"There are two great days in a person's life—the day we are born and the day we discover why."—William Barclay

When I was a kid, my dad told me celebrities in their twenties shouldn't write autobiographies. Their lives weren't long enough, and they hadn't experienced enough of the world.

I'm no celebrity, but here I am, writing my autobiography at nineteen years old. We all start as actors, and in time we become the authors of our own journey.

Age has never defined me, either. If anything, the numbers on my birth certificate became an asset to me. The old adage "good things come to those who wait" will never get a page in my book. Life, to me, is like fishing: you won't catch anything until you start, and every year you get older is another year the fish might slip through the net. And if you want to climb Everest, you'll need to sod the net and use a harpoon instead.

The courses dreams take, like disasters, are the result of particular chains of events that place obstacles in our way. All I know so far about the obstacles that make up life is that they are there to be overcome. It is the obstacles that make us grow.

I was born healthy, with every reason to be happy, in Chester on 18th June 1995. I felt lucky to be the only child of my parents, Debbie and Pete. After having me, they're probably relieved that there isn't a second child to worry about, too. All my life I've lived in the same modest house on a cul-de-sac in the leafy village of Kelsall, near Chester, United Kingdom. I can see the walls that were knocked down, and the way our home expanded and developed over the years, just like the foundations of my childhood.

How and why those foundations lead to me attempting to scale Mount Everest may not be obvious. This book is not a how-to guide on climbing Everest; it's a true story of how I refused to quit in pursuit of my goal, even amid tragedy and death.

Whilst there are many books about reaching the summit of the world, there are far less that tell the story of the two biggest disasters in Everest history. I think we learn more by losing than we do by winning—but by learning along the road, we cannot lose either way.

Why do we climb Everest? Perhaps it is the drive to live larger than life itself. I'm still not entirely sure. Carry on reading and let me know what you think. I've never been a great thinker; I'm a do-er, so writing this book has been my attempt to recollect and dissect this plethora of "doings" to discover how they led me to where I am today. Reflecting on exactly what has shaped us can reveal a lot about how we've been prepared for later life.

It may surprise you to learn that I wasn't the adventurous five-year-old always getting stuck in the neighbour's tree. In my younger years, my challenges were not self-inflicted like those I attempt today. I was not a borne adventurer, and although I had my share of obstacles, my upbringing varied little from that of most British children. I was fortunate to have so much and to be given the best chances in life, though I knew no different. Dad was a technical manager and Mum was a sales representative for a lighting company—perhaps that's how I got my sales skills. I grew up far from the mountains in a rural and hopelessly flat area of Cheshire with only forests and fields to explore. This undoubtedly had an influence on my love of the outdoors. Dad and I would go cycling in the forests occasionally, but he worked long hours, both away in China and in the office upstairs, so I spent most of my time with Mum. Whenever she took me shopping, I would scream until she was humiliated enough to take me home. I had my ways.

My grandparents, Norma and Derek, were a huge influence in my life. I visited them frequently at their home in Oldham, Manchester. Granddad was a gentle, modest, and caring man. He would take me to Manchester Airport to watch passenger jets take off and land from close up. Monotonous as this may sound, these trips inspired me to dream of becoming a pilot for many years, and perhaps also inspired my dream of exploring the world. My grandfather on the other side of the family passed away from cancer just eighteen months before I was born. It's sad that I never had chance to meet him, but he lives on in me every day through my middle name, Edward.

Neither I nor my family know why, but ever since I learnt to speak, my speech has been interrupted by a stammer, or stutter, as some describe it. Personally, I describe it as the bane of my life. When I started primary school, I would struggle to answer my name during the class register. I remember being taken to the hospital by ambulance soon after because I'd suffered a seizure under the living room table. No cause was found. Over a decade later, not much has changed. Some things in our life never will. The only solution is to learn to adapt to them. Adversity is the greatest teacher of all.

My free time was spent like any other kid trying to fit in: messing around with friends on homemade go-karts, making dens, terrorising the local residents with water pistols on long summer nights, and numbing my mind on whichever game console was in fashion at the time. Most Saturday nights, we indulged in a takeaway meal in front of the television. My parents were happy for me to do whatever I was happy doing.

I'd long despised exercise and would make any excuse to get out of it. One Sports Day at primary school I refused to play and threw an almighty tantrum just because my team was losing. The only sport that caught my interest was football. I became an avid Manchester United fan, and I would play football on Sunday mornings, but even with my weekly karate classes, I was terribly unfit. Back then, long walks could have me puffing for breath. Playing sports has never come naturally to me. Now, as an endurance athlete, I can train six days a week and still be outperformed by an easy-going guy in tight pants who lifts weights twice a week and drinks too much in the pub.

They say that a dog is truly a man's best friend and I guess that may be true. I had two dogs and they were a very important part of my life. I have vague memories of entering a barn to find adorable little chocolate Labrador puppies spilt like a bag of Maltesers across the carpet of straw. Hooch had grasped hold of Dad's jeans and wouldn't let go. So he chose us—and how lucky we were (although perhaps not so much our cats). With his barrel chest, huge paws, and brass collar, he resembled the slobbery French mastiff from the film *Turner & Hooch*.

We'd already had another chocolate Labrador, Harley. I remember playing outside in the garden the day my parents pulled up the drive with a brown dog wearing sunglasses sitting on Mum's knee. I still don't know why Harley was wearing sunglasses, but he'd been named after one of Dad's motorbikes. Both dogs were like the brothers I never had, and their love was unconditional. I wish I'd been able to take them in the mountains. Nowadays, I carry photos of them on my expeditions and vow to bring one to the top of the world.

Certain moments and feelings in life can never be replicated. For me, those moments were walking the dogs on autumnal Sunday afternoons. On weekends we would take our caravan to the Isle of Anglesey in Wales. In the gale-force winds we'd hibernate with hot chocolate and fish & chips as rain pummeled the windows, or we'd take the dogs down to swim in Red Wharf Bay with sand between our toes. I feel a tinge of sadness when I recall our holidays to southern France—the freshly baked croissants, the archery practice, and the fishing trips, which became my favourite hobby for many years. At the time, I rarely saw more adrenalin than the thrill of riding my bike or the excitement of catching my first common carp, for which Dad had leapt chest-deep into a pond to grab the end of my fishing rod before it sunk into the depths—along with his phone and wallet.

These simple times were the happiest I knew. Before we learn that becoming an astronaut is extremely unlikely, we all have our childhood dreams. We cannot make them all a reality, which is fine, but that is no excuse for dreaming small. We just have to prioritise the ambitions that mean most to us. Many people often dream of returning to a conventional form of living, minus the pressures and commitments. As time passed, I would begin to make decisions to avoid the influences that tried to shape me to fit the mould. Today, I rebel against the conveyor belt system of society to the utmost of my ability. You have to possess a stubborn belief in an idea to make it reality—but I could never have imagined where mine would take me. I only knew that if you follow the same beaten path, you're probably going to end up in the same place.

CHAPTER 2

Man of the House

"Being challenged in life is inevitable, being defeated is optional."—Roger Crawford

I was a sensitive, pessimistic, and sophisticated kid. I wasn't the most popular, nor was I the class loner. My self-confidence had cracks. Whilst I can readily take risks to make my dreams a reality, my passive character was easily overpowered. I still struggle to make eye contact with people whilst speaking, or to make a simple phone call. As I grew up, I was neither the strongest nor the smartest, although I was proud of what academic talent I had. Known as a teacher's pet, I thrived on praise and attention, especially from Dad. My parents were never sparse with their encouragement. They were proud of me and pushed me along to achieve. On one occasion, after achieving glowing scores on the SATs, I remember Mum pretending to be angry as though I'd performed badly; when I began to sob, she was guilt-stricken.

Until later experiences taught me that there was more to life, I was a perfectionist, perpetually frustrated by what I saw as my failure to live up to my own high standards. Some of those traits remain wired inside me today. In time, I would grow more disappointed with my lack of success in everyday tasks than the more important, character-building endeavours that depended mostly on objective factors.

When I was seven, I suffered another seizure in my parents' office; on waking, I couldn't remember anything. Two years later, a terrifying seizure occurred for no reason as I was eating a McDonald's takeaway in the car. My eyes retracted into the back of my head so I appeared to be staring at nothing until I came round. These instances were distressing for those who could only observe, especially Mum. The seizures became a massive trigger for my anxiety. It was years before I'd touch fast food again, and even salty smells could send my mind into overdrive, increase my heart rate, and leave me so light-headed I had to sit down. At a very impressionable age, I was mostly occupied with strategies for keeping calm, which tainted much of the enjoyment of my childhood.

Seizures and their knock-on effects to my wellbeing also dogged my achievements in the classroom. During my final year of primary school, I suffered a huge one, conscious only of waking sick and disorientated, my vision a hazy yellow as I lay beneath a desk in the Biology classroom. My classmates had been horrified by my piercing screams. The few months that followed were unsettled as I became afraid to leave the house unless my parents were nearby. Although I looked ordinary on the outside, I struggled to feel safe anywhere. I was paralysed by the thought of never knowing when another seizure could strike and traumatised by throwing up en route to the hospital, anxious about the tests I had to undergo. Full-on panic attacks were a regular occurrence too, usually in public places, like on one occasion after a petit mal seizure—a total loss of awareness for around twenty seconds—whilst eating out at a restaurant with my family.

The eventual diagnosis was a brain condition called epilepsy. I'm still haunted by the childish terror of the claustrophobic tunnel where the MRI scanner boomed in my ears; I trembled so badly the scan had to be repeated. A number of scans failed to locate the origin or confirm the type of seizure, although fortunately it appeared to take a mild form. It wasn't photosensitive, but when we had school photos taken I refused and ran away from the flash anyway. My consultant Dr. Jayaram prescribed medication that could be sprinkled onto my toast each morning, but it took months of Mum refusing to let me out of her sight, or allowing me to have baths, to get the medication right.

Since coming off this medication, I am fortunate not to have experienced another seizure. I know it could return at any point and put an indefinite stop to what I do, but I cannot live in fear. Nevertheless, actually dealing with epilepsy catalysed many other obstacles that impacted my young life and made me who I am today. After developing a phobia of hospitals and needles, and a consequent wish to avoid them, I became a hypochondriac health fanatic. I thought that sprinting up and down the nearest field would make myself stronger and less vulnerable, although it probably didn't do much for my fitness.

My epilepsy and "stutter mouth" made me extremely nervous about starting Tarporley Community High in 2006, and one morning in my first week, I threw up all over the floor of the school bus. Nearly everyone experiences bullying in their life, but without telling a sob story, school was never easy for me. Whilst I grew up disproportionately through adolescence into the lanky six-foot-four-inches tall that I now stand, I had a noticeably large head. That was all the other kids needed. "Big head" became the most common insult, but they had a wide selection for when they got bored. Whilst I write this, I laugh at how meaningless these words are, but as a teenager, it felt otherwise. This frequent abuse became humiliating and scarred my already-compromised self-confidence even further, and my frustrated retaliation didn't do me any favours.

Our school had a pointless tradition of making all of the first-years run a one-mile cross country race in front of the older students around the school field. I finished third to last, humiliated at how unfit I was. Rugby classes were even worse, as I was usually paired up with a gargantuan kid called Tom Jennings who must have weighed double what I did. Other kids would convince him that I'd called him names so that he would try and hurt me in retaliation.

Starting secondary school was difficult for other reasons: at that time, my parents were going through an overdue and difficult divorce. Parents Evening, which they both had to attend, marooned me in a growing rift, under incredible strain not to take sides. Inevitably I was dragged into the backlash; the change of routine unsettled me and left me to try to come to terms with the events on my own. I adopted the role of man of the house, which matured me more quickly than it should have. Instead of being carefree, I developed obsessive-compulsive disorder during my teenage years, and my anxiety grew even worse. For years I struggled to sleep at night, worried about everything from fire to burglars, and I saw it as my duty to walk around the house several times, checking that doors were locked and appliances had been switched off. These triggers came in phases that petered away in time.

Nevertheless, the divorce brought out Mum's fighting spirit, something else I believe I have inherited from her. Mum is seldom adventurous and generally appreciative of simpler things, like a glass of wine or three. She surprised us when her favourite pastime became riding a Yamaha jet ski. Mum is short and stubborn, with a huge mop of curly blonde hair that she is always trying to get rid of. Her bubbly character and subtle sense of humour always shines through.

As she fought to make ends meet and keep the same roof over our heads, Dad moved in with a new girlfriend, also named Debbie. I will never understand how Mum coped with it. She was quietly driven and devoted to everyone around her. All she wanted was the best for me and the dogs. We managed, made our own memories, and we made the house our own. As dreary winter nights crept in and the streetlights flickered to life, I would walk the dogs every day, like Dad always had, without fail.

I can remember our very first Christmas alone, and it was fun: heaving a tree into the back of the car, howling with laughter as chestnuts exploded in the oven. With the tins of Quality Street chocolates and the long, frosty walks, it remained my favourite time of year. Most nights, I went overboard in an effort to help Mum by making dinner and occasionally trying her patience with three-course meals. Civil wars between cornflour and the cooker were a frequent occurrence. I worked obsessively on the garden and when a dead rat was found in our pond, it was my job to fling it over the fence with a spade. On New Year's Eve, I extinguished a candle with what I thought was water but was actually alcohol, sending a cascade of flames up the living room wall and charring the ceiling.

I felt keenly the weight of these new responsibilities—but I had a lot to learn.

CHAPTER 3

Growing Wings

"Life is ten percent what you experience and ninety percent how you respond to it."—Dorothy M. Neddermeyer

We all have our fears. Anyone who says otherwise is probably scared of admitting it.

Driven by the fear of more seizures, my anxiety latched onto anything it could. Somehow I never had any therapy, apart from the school nurse I talked to. I have always tried to learn to cope by myself, perhaps so I don't become a burden on anybody else. All it took was reading one newspaper article about the dangers of the solvents in body sprays and I'd be running out of the room before I had a panic attack or trying to calm down at my desk as my vision blurred and the room whirled around me. Kids, being kids, would chase me to deliberately spray it in my face. Many of the teachers were powerless, or useless, to stop it.

My skin thickened when I found a small group of similarly-outcast friends to pass the time with, and playing my guitar at lunchtimes was an escape. Learning "Back in Black" by AC/DC on Dad's Fender Stratocaster made rock music the soundtrack of my life. My first proper "band" was a two-piece with my friend Tom on drums. We unimaginatively named ourselves "Black Ice" after the AC/DC album. Shy by nature but kind-hearted and outspoken, Tom is one of only two people from high school whom I still keep in regular contact with. In the coming years, I stopped taking lessons and taught myself to play bass guitar, keyboard, and drums, though my impatience and perfectionism prevented me from becoming any good. I have always had various interests, a jack of all trades and master of none. Like many high school students, one of my dreams was to play a killer gig in school—another dream that never happened. We got no-where, learning only two songs in two years, but it was good fun. My other best friend at school was Sam. We enjoyed plenty of boyish mischief; one prank involved lacing his younger sister's hot chocolate with Tabasco sauce, which ended up splattering their parents' white curtains and carpet when she shrieked and threw the drink all over him. Even though with Sam I was able to relax and be myself, every day at school felt like a summons to the firing squad, taunts fol-lowing me everywhere and my friends rarely standing up for me.

On the twenty-five-minute bus ride home, other kids would sing chants, make gestures from the pavements out-side, and come over with a ruler to measure my head. One particular afternoon, someone had stolen my sports kitbag, so I left my guitar in its case on the pavement whilst I went back on to retrieve it. Unprovoked as usual, a hefty older boy started to kick the guitar beneath the bus just before it drove off. I tried to stick up for myself but was thrown against the side of the bus and punched until I was unconscious and bleeding. Mum went berserk and rang the school. She was fiercely protective of her family, never one to give up easily, whereas I quit my karate lessons shortly after. I was only one belt below receiving my black belt, but felt it had served me no benefit whatsoever.

It was hard to stick up for myself with a stammer. Stammering is not just an annoying repetition of words, but also causes complete blocks where I cannot pronounce a sin-gle word and pull twisted facial expressions—like my classic "flycatcher"—where my mouth is open but no sound comes out. You could say it's like having an invisible ball at the back of your throat that keeps getting stuck. I have to replace certain trigger words with others that flow more easily, creating some ad-hoc sentences that often don't make sense. The worst is when I'm unable to say my own name. How can I possibly pretend that I've forgotten my name? Because of one red-faced occasion, baristas at my local coffee shop write the name "Matt" on my cup, as that was the only name I could pronounce at the time. I just have to go along with it.

All this probably explains why I'm still socially awkward, but my stammer was the biggest culprit. Even going to the shop filled me with dread, in case someone spoke to me and I was unable to respond. I hated to think they might perceive me as rude or ignorant; I always know exactly what I want to say, which is where the frustration lies. At social events I would take my laptop and tuck myself away in the corner to avoid contact. Even before I was old enough to buy alcohol, I decided I'd never get married because I'd never be able to say my vows.

I have always enjoyed writing, probably because I have never been able to express myself by speaking. Still, English classes at school were the worst because it meant reading out loud so everyone else could hear me. I feared being judged, and it was frustrating that I was unable to do something that everybody else took for granted. I often skipped class to avoid these lessons. Countless hours of my first year were spent in the reception pretending to be ill, and my flamboyant acting usually meant I got away with it.

If you visit a zoo, you'll observe the inevitable clashing of personalities where weaknesses are exposed, a bit like survival of the fittest. You can spot at least one of each species in the group. School was no different. Young people are pushed through the same system just when we're trying to understand life, decide what's important to us, and discover who we are—we all wanted to make our mark on the world. In those first years, I started to notice my friends changing rapidly around me. Even though I knew it was an inevitable part of growing up, it made me sad. Sam, too, was sucked into the latest trends when I just wanted to mess around with a football like we always had.

Many spent their time trying to impress people who were not worth impressing, whilst others differentiated themselves to gain attention by dressing like a member of a seventies heavy metal band or slathering on enough fake tan to play an Oompa Loompa in *Willie Wonka & the Chocolate Factory.* I can describe it best as "monkey see, monkey do"— fortunately, the metaphorical monkey on my shoulder would soon do a runner.

Eventually, I was unknowingly swayed by social expectations. Changing to please my new friends was different, but I finally felt more respected and less like a victim. Life became as normal as I'd known it so far. This false security gave me no immunity, though, when at a friend's birthday party I suffered a major panic attack.

A new camera I received for Christmas gave me some independence and inspired me to begin taking photographs of the wild birds in my garden. Wandering around the countryside for hours studying the harmony of nature with twigs crunching beneath my feet became ridiculously exciting. My love of the outdoors had been brewing longer than I probably realised. As a child, my grandma and I would watch wildlife together from the conservatory, and her compassion and love of nature were clearly instilled in me. Animals were no different from humans in her eyes. She always told me that everything was put on this planet for a reason. Gran was responsible for my emotional investment in global warming, and the devastation that humanity was inflicting on the world bothered me greatly. Watching a TV program about the Sea Shepherd, an environmental organisation fighting whaling in the Arctic, caught me especially hard. The callous murder of wildlife boiled my blood and put me off fishing. I felt an overwhelming affinity with their passion, the way they got their hands dirty and risked their lives for what they believed in without the flower-power shorts, and I wanted to be out there fighting, too.

It was the first time I decided that life needed a purpose—not just to breathe air and put nothing back. I hoped to be remembered for my contribution to the world and the things I achieved. I was not going to preach and inspire the masses, at least not for a while, but change was exciting, and it seemed to my young eyes that this would be the most satiating path a person could take to be truly successful. For similar reasons, one of my life's ambitions is to receive a knighthood; not for the bragging rights, but to have solid proof that I have made a significant contribution to our planet.

In the meantime, I began looking for more realistic ways to help. A few stressful months of self-taught web design later, Cheshire Wildlife Group, a website with my photography, blogs, and tips on how to help protect local and global habitats, went online. When the government announced a cull of badgers in the countryside, I was angry and determined to do what I could to stop the slaughter of wildlife. I printed posters all over my village and emailed every single member of the House of Lords in British Parliament to express my views. My passion was the sort of thing I was scared to admit to my new friends. They bored me anyway. I gradually lost interest to follow my purpose, and something innocuous nibbled away at me.

My first holiday alone with Mum was to Letoonia Resort, nestled amongst an idyllic peninsula near the town of Fethiye, Turkey. I loved spending afternoons rocking on hammocks, floating along the beach in an inflatable ring, swimming in the pools, winding up the Russian tourists, and conquering the all-inclusive restaurant buffet each day. We always had a laugh together. Mum persuaded me to try a scuba diving taster day, and I soon found myself on a little dive boat off the coast of Marmaris with an unsettled stomach—but not from seasickness. For once, the thought of a panic attack failed to cross my mind whilst exploring the topaz lagoons with an instructor by my side. Diving was a fabulous and invigorating sensation. I had always been interested in marine life and dreamt of being a marine biologist for a long time, although I remembered vividly how I cried in despair to my tutor at school, Mr. Edwards, because my squeamishness made the required Biology A-Level classes too much to cope with. Although I did eventually get an A-Level in Biology (having spent numerous classes in the corridor to avoid passing out), diving seemed a much better way to explore marine fauna.

Inspired by the sensation of adrenalin, a little wooden kiosk advertising tandem paragliding caught my eye. A strange and unexplainable urge replaced the apprehension within my thirteen-year-old self, and I decided that I was going to try it. Mum seemed both uneasy and a little shocked at where this sudden drive had come from. Perhaps this self-conscription stemmed from the fact that I hated regrets and forever guilted myself for mistakes and missed chances, something I had probably learnt from stammering. Conquering fear, I learnt, was usually as straightforward as weighing up everything and giving myself no other realistic choice but to do the things I was afraid of.

My flight was booked for the morning after, so I couldn't change my mind. The next day I couldn't touch my breakfast, a sure sign something was untoward. Vacuum-packed into an old Jeep, we rattled up the side of Mount Babadag on a coarse mountain track through pine forests and precarious edges, a cloud of dust rising behind us.

"Are you sure you want to do this?" Mum asked apprehensively.

I doubted it. I felt sick and asked my instructor numerous naïve questions, thinking I was going to die. Before I knew it, we were harnessed together, and I stood jelly-legged at the top of a paved slope above the clouds, baking in the sun. There was no backing out now. I was told to run. I wanted to run the other way. Those few seconds had the power to change my life.

*Paragliding in Olu Deniz, Turkey. Unlocking the
confidence I never knew I had.*

A sudden gust caught the paraglider, hurling the towel-
width material upwards, pulling the wires taut, and unfolding it like eagle wings. We swooped into the air like the butterflies in my churning stomach. I opened my eyes again. As
we soared effortlessly in the thermals for forty minutes, dangling over the intense blue of the Olu Deniz lagoon, I eased
back and relaxed. The hotel swimming pools shrank to
speckles of dust six thousand feet below my trainers, and I
had never felt such freedom or pride. The drive and confidence that had been locked inside me for all those years escaped into the mountain breeze and blew away like a feather.
I was sure I had found where I belonged.

As we glided down to land, I felt like I could do anything I put my mind to. Discovering this was like opening a
gateway to a new galaxy of potential. I felt like a boxer who
had regained consciousness and was ready to knock out all
my opponents. I decided I wasn't going to be a victim anymore.

CHAPTER 4

Where is Mount Everest?

"When you go to the mountains, you see them and you admire them. In a sense, they give you a challenge, and you try to express that challenge by climbing them."
—*Sir Edmund Hillary*

I came back to school an entirely different student—and to an even larger round of mockery—but I finally started to care more for what I believed in than what others thought of me. After being victimised all my life, I enjoyed having the courage to defy the mould. Increasingly, I began to struggle getting on with people my own age, but at the time I didn't think it acceptable to class adults as friends. Nowadays, most of my friends are at least a decade older than me. True friendship really shines once you learn that age doesn't matter.

In March 2010, Dad and my stepmum took me to Fort William in Scotland. As soon as we crossed the border, I was mesmerised by the snow-capped pine forests, the monstrous lochs, and the imposing mountain forts. "Everlong" by the Foo Fighters, my favourite song, blasted in my ears and gave me energy. For three hours I pointed at every peak and asked whether it could be Ben Nevis, the highest mountain in the

United Kingdom. I was lucky to even make it to the campsite.

This would be my first proper mountain, and I was ecstatic at the prospect of the climb when we headed up a couple of days later. The walk was strenuous work, and the rest of the family were considerably less enthusiastic. But again, my imagination melted into the iridescent blue skies and icy chill of the March breeze as I took it all in, feasting my eyes on the scale of the landscape and towering mountain strongholds. Further up the path, the snow began to deepen. Dad and I trudged through alone. The Ben Nevis tourist track has huge drop-offs where a slip could send you hurtling back to Glen Nevis in a hurry, and without crampons and ice axes we weren't suitably equipped for the winter conditions. I remember assessing the loaded slopes around me for risks the whole time. Considering I had about as much mountain experience as the people in jeans and trainers following us, this was quite distressing. The skill of risk assessment came naturally to me at fourteen years old.

Whilst disappointed, I made the call and insisted we turn around before the summit. Taking leadership and responsibility struck a chord with me. That moment became one of the most significant of my mountaineering career.

With growing confidence, I decided I'd finally had enough of the torment on the school bus and decided to cycle the five miles to school on my ancient mountain bike. I never went back. The journey was surprisingly easy, with scenic views of the rolling Cheshire countryside, and I was only ten minutes slower than the old buses. Even after the winter rain made the roads icy and the mornings dark, I persevered. I was unafraid to be different, the only student to cycle to school. My fitness improved drastically, but biking did have some drawbacks. Rocks and glass bottles were sometimes launched at me from the pavements, and on three occasions, frothy splodges of spit hit me from passing buses and cars. After receiving some jibes the next day, I came out of class to find my bike tyres slashed; it felt like the whole world was laughing at me.

I took a summer job at our village garden centre watering plants and building sheds in order to fund a new bike and more outdoor pursuits. Once that job finished I started working at a local pub as a kitchen porter, a glorified term for pot washer. The Royal Oak was great fun, though the world of work took some getting used to. If I didn't feel I had worked hard enough on my shifts, I would write my hours down incorrectly so I would be underpaid accordingly. Eventually I realised that I had to support myself too. The banter made it worthwhile, throwing snowballs across the kitchen and being chased by the chefs with tea-towels. I was regularly doubled over the sink with laughter at the vulgar comebacks they suggested I use against the bullies. When the business went under a few months later, I felt I'd lost a community.

I've learned two things about bullying: firstly, nobody can *make* you feel bad—it is your decision how you respond. Secondly, it is hugely beneficial to maintain eye contact. My size had never intimidated the bullies because I walked around with my head down. Keeping my shoulders strong and my eyes forward made a world of difference.

Now I had the courage to not only try new things, but to stand up to the bullies. One morning, one of the culprits repeated the jibes. I punched him cleanly in the chin. He staggered backwards with tears in his eyes and shuffled off down the corridor. He never said a word again.

Anybody who proposes that the best method for dealing with bullies is to simply ignore them has most likely never been bullied. After all, advice is only a reflection of another person's perspective, and from my extensive experience, bullying usually occurs due to boredom, jealousy, or insecurities in the bullies themselves. A rare few are just born with a shortage of brain cells, and you can't help but feel sorry for them. Hopefully some of the aggressors are reading this book now with remorse, having learnt from their mistakes and become respectful members of the community. Otherwise, I would politely recommend they use this book to forcefully whack that big furry spider on their forehead.

After Ben Nevis, I was itching to get back outside again and find what I could overcome next. Shortly after, my friend Tom invited me on holiday to the Lake District with his family, who were keen hill-walkers. At first I was anxious, but Mum convinced me to go, for which I will be forever thankful.

Typically, we started in drizzly rain. I trudged along paths through bracken and entertained myself counting the sheep in the village of Mungrisdale. I don't think anybody really enjoys walking uphill, the unfortunate fact being that the further you go, the further you have still to come down. But as the clouds suddenly lifted, we topped out on Souther Fell—my first English fell—and I knew where the enjoyment came from. Neil, Tom's stepdad, pointed out the tooth-like saddle of Blencathra and the jagged shoulders of neighbouring peaks on the horizon; the Himalayas could have been in my windscreen for all I knew. Sitting beneath these giants to eat my lunch was so rewarding. I gazed around and felt my breath being carried away.

At one point during this fateful day, I thought to myself, where is Mount Everest? I didn't know where that question came from. Neil explained it was on the border between Nepal and Tibet, but I wanted to know more.

That night, I started to research online. At 29,029 feet above sea-level, or 8,848 metres, her summit was near the cruising height of a modern jetliner. The peak stood within the Mahalangur region of the Himalayas, the highest mountain range in the world. Everest was named after the British surveyor Sir George Everest in 1865 and British mountaineers had been the first to attempt to reach the summit. In Nepal it was known as Sagarmatha, and in Tibet as Chomolungma, meaning "Goddess Mother of Mountains." I thought the Tibetan interpretation seemed more appropriate. Her precipices, depths, and ice cathedrals enthralled me. The sheer scale of the Himalayan peaks was beyond my imagination and incomparable to anything I had seen before. Images flashed in my mind and raised the hair on my arms. I could think of no place more incredible in the world.

I discovered that regular people had managed to climb to the top, where only one-third of the oxygen at sea level was available. On the *Everest 1953—The British Story* website, I found a list of all the British Everest summiteers, and however ordinary, they seemed superhuman to me. Less than four thousand people had succeeded, and her slopes had become the final resting place of over two hundred. It intimidated and empowered me at once. The statistics were frightening, but I wanted nothing more than to get my name on that list, to earn a place in this elite group. I wanted to achieve something substantial, and that was Everest. Reaching the summit had become the ultimate obstacle, the biggest thing to overcome. Somehow I even thought that this moment might bring my nirvana. To reach my potential on the pinnacle of the world suddenly meant everything to me. It was all I could ever want.

Most of me doubted that my plans would make it to breakfast the following morning. Perhaps my mid-life crisis had come prematurely. But I promised myself I would follow through. At some point everyone feels the thrill of possibility within, but many ignore it for fear of disappointment. I wouldn't. A long and winding road had officially begun— one that would bring far more than I could have ever bargained for.

PART 2

DISCOVERY

CHAPTER 5

Getting High

"To be yourself in a world that is constantly trying to make you something else is the greatest accomplishment."—Ralph Waldo Emerson

Term started again and I studied hard in preparation for my exams. I chose four subjects for my GCSE grades—Geography, Business Studies, Music and Food Technology—the last two purely for fun. Academically I was still performing well, but I grew despondent from hanging around with friends. I had better ways to invest my time. My break times were spent at a computer working on my website, wildlife campaigning, and quenching my fascination for Everest in any way I could. The mountain was like an itch I couldn't scratch. Through further research I found a rock climbing instructor and Everest summiteer, Tim Mosedale, and I decided I had to meet him.

My challenges outdoors became more than just a hobby. The desire was more than a thirst for adventure. It came from a will to live the most meaningful life I could. It was my escape, my way of looking adversity straight in the eye. Undeniably, I also longed to wipe the smiles off the bullies' faces, to show them I had the courage to venture into the unknown. Every new challenge filled me with excitement and fulfilment that I could not get from my daily life. Everest symbolised the highest high I could reach.

I felt I was making up for lost time and every second counted. I had more ideas than I could keep up with, and I wanted to cram in as much as possible. Doing things by halves was no longer an option.

My interest in fitness developed along with my interest in the outdoors. Dad was very fit, having run for years and completed numerous London marathons in respectable times. Earlier that year in France, my stepmum Debbie had bet two pounds that I wouldn't go on a run with him. I couldn't refuse the challenge. For thirty minutes or so, I suffered, sweated, and wheezed. When we got there, I proudly indulged in pain au chocolat with my earnings.

I first discovered the thrill of competition when I entered a ten-kilometre race for charity months later. I loved the reward of returning home from the soggy rain with the new mental strength I gained from exercise. Many people, myself included, cannot understand how exercise can bring immense pleasure until they try it. I learnt doing things that challenge our bodies can actually make us feel wonderfully alive. I had neglected my health for a long time, but now I struggle to imagine my life without exercise. Only when we discover this can we truly enjoy the comforts of life without the self-contempt of sitting on the sofa and saying, "I'll go to the gym tomorrow."

I was always running in our local forest. When the government tried to privatise it a year later, I plastered about twenty posters over the office window of my local politician. I became so involved that I nearly failed my first exams because I was focused on being a spokesperson for a local campaign team. But still, we won, and the bid was thrown out—as was I from the campaign team. I decided to stick with fundraising, for now at least. But all of my campaigning had connected me to people who shared my beliefs. Andy was a cheerful soul, a charity fundraiser in his late twenties, and Barbara was an acupuncturist who invited me on the group hill-walks she organised. Those weekends spent exploring Snowdonia only increased my outdoor ambitions further.

I was standing in the shower when the idea of doing the National Three Peaks Challenge came to me from nowhere. The Three Peaks involves climbing the three highest mountains in the UK in less than twenty-four hours. I researched what had been done previously and resolved to climb the mountains solo, which, at sixteen years old, would make me the youngest person ever to achieve this.

My aunt had recently recovered from breast cancer, so I wanted to support a charity called Breakthrough Breast Cancer. I also decided to support a charity called REACT (Red Endangered Animal Connection Trust), which supported wildlife conservation, particularly orangutans and endangered species in Borneo. Raising money for charity through my challenges made sense. Through my new passion I found compassion.

One October morning we drove up to Keswick, the capital of the Lake District, where I finally met Tim Mosedale. Tim had achieved something that I still couldn't comprehend. Everest climbers were my role models, not celebrities; whilst I had always felt different because of my stammer and epilepsy, they were different for a remarkable reason. I was excited to meet an Everest climber for the first time, but my first day of rock climbing was a daunting prospect.

Those first crawls up the weathered walls of Shepherds Crag were hard but rewarding. Clinging to the side of the rock, I assessed each lip and crack before grasping. I felt free like a gymnast, both challenged and focused, moving with increasing confidence as the rope tightened reassuringly after each move. My self-doubt fell away the higher I climbed. Finally we reached the top of Brown Slabs, where Tim congratulated me on my first-ever rock climb.

We finished the day with the route Little Chamonix, where you belay—the practice of securing your climbing partner with a rope—from a rocky saddle high above the treetops. This may not sound enjoyable, but I was awestruck. Being out on the edge released my inhibitions, and for a moment I forgot all my worries. I realised that conquering fear could be immensely satisfying and fulfilling.

I didn't stop talking the whole day, picking Tim's brain to see how I could follow in his footsteps. Learning from his experiences on Everest both intimidated and enticed me. I knew I would get there; it was not if, but when. I wish I'd realised that there would be no way back. I was still Alex, the same person in the same house with the same family, but my attitude had completely changed.

CHAPTER 6

Baby Steps

"Dreams, though, are cheap, and the real task comes when you start putting in place the steps needed to make those dreams a reality."—Bear Grylls

By July, the Three Peaks Challenge was fast approaching. My stepdad Chris, a taxi driver, had volunteered to drive straight away. Mum and Chris had got married earlier that year. He was slightly younger than her, but since she had struggled on her own for so long I was glad to see her happy again, and it took some of the responsibilities off my shoulders. He looked after her and wanted the best for both of us.

Chris owned his own business, Tarvin Cars, and eventually mum started working as a taxi driver too. His eight-seat minibus was especially useful as we set off for Scotland. Whilst he would drive, I would walk the mountains alone. I had walked all three before, but I was apprehensive. Friends and family doubted whether I could do it, but I tried not to listen. I'd learnt everything about the logistics and the organisation that I could. This was the biggest thing I'd ever taken on.

That evening I raced up Ben Nevis, the peak that had bested Dad and I the year before. I made it back to the car park ahead of schedule and with a proud smile on my face.

Everything was going to plan so far. After several hours in the minibus we arrived at the second peak, Scafell Pike. I wasted no time hurtling up the steps of the footpath in the blue-tinged dawn. Navigating was difficult, and I got lost for a while in the mist crowning the summit, but soon enough I was back in the minibus.

We were well ahead of time with a comfortable margin to complete the final peak, Snowdon, in Wales. Seeing the rock looming in the windscreen didn't faze me; seeing my plans unfolding like clockwork was a sure sign I had a knack for this. On my descent from Snowdon, I remembered something Dad had told me about running—to slow down if I needed or walk if I had to, so long as I didn't stop.

An older man stopped me on the path after noticing the shirt advertising my challenge. He was leading three teenage girls on their own Three Peaks attempt and asked my age out of interest. After I told him, he grinned and shook my hand.

"You better keep going then!" he said.

I jogged the final couple of miles and finished in under twenty-two hours.

Only Mum and Chris were waiting at the Pen-y-Pass car park, and that was enough. We celebrated with photos as I became the youngest person ever to walk the three mountains alone within the twenty-four hour limit. On reflection, this was a pretty insignificant record. But stretched out on the drive home, I couldn't care less. It was a wonderful feeling of satisfaction, progress, and achievement. And the responses I received were even better. It gave me a feeling I had almost forgotten: self-worth.

We raised 1,800 pounds for the charities and I was chuffed to bits. This sum was mostly achieved by pestering people with sponsor forms until they had no excuse, though I would later discover that this card could only be played once or twice, and I'd have to think more creatively if I was to continue raising funds through my challenges.

Later, the record for the Three Peaks Challenge was taken by a younger student at my school, which says a lot about

Alex and his stepdad after the Three Peaks Challenge.

the power of inspiration. After all, records were made to be broken.

The summer of 2011 was the best of my life, mostly because I got to leave high school. With my wages I bought a brand new Specialized Rockhopper mountain bike. Riding the trails at sunset with the Foo Fighters blasting in my ears made me happier than I had been in a long time. I would cycle to the village of Frodsham, about eleven miles away, and go bouldering on the sandstone crags concealed in the forest, a form of climbing without ropes that focuses on solving "problems" on the rock.

I also loved walking the dogs in Primrose Wood, a pine forest on a nearby hill. Hidden deep within was a sandstone gorge called Urchins Kitchen where I loved to practice the moves in my climbing magazines.

One day, my dog Hooch peered down at me from above, having found his own way up. He stood on the edge of the crag, threatening to make the jump from about fifteen feet, and absolutely loving his game.

"Don't you dare!" I ordered.

Harley and Hooch

He tilted his head sarcastically. This dog was not normal.

We went back to Turkey on holiday, and this time I became a qualified PADI Open Water scuba diver. Even though I forgot to inflate my buoyancy jacket, plummeted to the seabed, and spit out my breathing regulator on the final day, I managed to pass my course. I was able to scuba dive with sharks at Blue Planet Aquarium back home for my seventeenth birthday.

It didn't take long to find my next big challenge, and I emailed a guiding company, Dream Guides, to express my interest in Everest. The clerk in the office replied with a suggested itinerary of milestones that would build my mountaineering resume and prepare me for Everest. All I had was UK hill-walking and climbing experience, so the first of these stepping stones would be to climb Mont Blanc, the highest peak in the Alps. I signed myself up for the following summer. Many people have dreams, but few take the steps to actually make them a reality. A lack of self-confidence was definitely not going to get in the way of mine.

CHAPTER 7

Leaps and Bounds

"Our greatest glory is not in never falling, but in rising every time we fall."—Confucius

After high school, I stayed on at sixth form college to study A-Levels, probably because I didn't know what I wanted to do besides climb Everest. A-Levels were a drag.

Soon I began working at The Boot Inn, a hearty little pub down the road. I was working as many hours as I could to pay for my Mont Blanc trip, which would cost about two thousand pounds. Washing dishes every weekend worked for now, but I had no idea how I would finance my Everest expedition.

It seemed that every challenge came with even more hidden challenges, until one day I received a Facebook message from Becky Bellworthy, a nineteen-year-old British girl from Hampshire who had read about my Three Peaks Challenge and wanted to congratulate me. I learned she had just returned from her first attempt to summit Everest, falling short due to a serious medical emergency at Camp Two. Becky had funded her Everest expedition through corporate sponsorship. Her encouragement would become the most significant message I had ever received. She gave me hope that perhaps one day it might happen for me too. Becky achieved her dream one year later when she stood on top of the world, aged just twenty years old.

Sponsorship still seemed daunting and remote. In an attempt to secure sponsors, I sent a poorly conceived letter to local companies that I would be ashamed to reveal to anyone nowadays. Nevertheless, if school taught me anything, it was how to do my research. As my physics teacher, Mr. Stone, used to say, "The test is easy—if you know the answers!" I think he was onto something.

I interrogated Becky and two other British climbers on her expedition, Matthew Dieumegard-Thornton and Mollie Hughes, to learn as much as possible. One of the earliest bits of advice they gave me was to set up a website about myself. I knew I needed someone with actual web design skills. I'd recently competed in Hellrunner, the UK's toughest half marathon, which involved freezing waist-deep bogs, obstacles, and numerous laps of sustained hills. During the race I'd ran past a bloke wearing nothing but an authentic Borat mankini. Somehow we connected on Facebook, and when I searched for a free website designer, Chris offered his help straight away. A keen runner in his twenties, he continues to maintain my website today, but has since retired the mankini. I developed a supportive team through other such coincidental meetings.

My local newspaper, the Chester Chronicle, was always raising awareness of my challenges, so often that it was almost embarrassing. Thanks to them, I received another message from a local girl, Lauren, who had read the news article about my Three Peaks Challenge after completing it herself. She was also seventeen, and we got on well. A few weeks later, I asked her to go mountain biking with me in Delamere Forest. Even paragliding wasn't as terrifying as that morning. She became my first girlfriend, and I was smitten. We hiked in the mountains, ran a half marathon together, and even went to the cinema. To hell with the conventional dinner dates, I thought, and she was adventurous too. Time wasting had never been so enjoyable. It was innocent fun, or at least it was for me.

It lasted a pretty pathetic two months until she broke my heart with a Facebook message one December night. I ran home through the wood like Forrest Gump, and even ran twenty miles the next day.

Your first breakup is always the most painful, an overwhelming feeling of sadness and loss. Mine triggered other negative feelings and insecurities I had dealt with over the years. Feeling rejected and helpless was something I knew well, but this was like nothing else. Running became my coping mechanism, and nothing felt worthwhile anymore. Pounding the tarmac was the only thing that could lift my mood, but even then, I always seemed to fall back down. It seemed I would never feel lighter. Soon I was unable to study for more than five minutes without my head cradled hopelessly in my hands. I even refused to peel myself out of bed on Christmas Day.

Mum eventually took me to the doctor, where I realised this melancholy had a name: depression. After everything I'd been through, I was disappointed that such a silly event could knock me for six. But progress is like a jigsaw; the pieces don't always fall into place in the way we hope they might. Giving it a label made it somewhat easier to manage, but in the long term made it harder because I was always on guard.

By a stroke of good timing, I joined West Cheshire Athletics Club and competed in the ten-kilometre events, often cycling home from sixth form to run eleven miles there and back again. Sprinting and training six days a week helped stifle my sorrows.

The track wasn't the only thing I'd be running around, as I discovered one day while checking my emails. My heart nearly jumped through the roof.

"Congratulations—we think you've got what it takes to be a London 2012 Olympic Torchbearer!" I punched the air, unable to contain my excitement. Ecstatic didn't come close.

Only eight thousand people had been chosen to carry the Olympic Flame ahead of the London 2012 Olympic Games opening ceremony, and I would be one of them. The Torch Relay is the ceremonial relaying of the flame from Olympia, Greece, to the site of an Olympic Games. Normally it only involved athletes, celebrities, and notable figures, so what the hell was I doing as part of it?

For London 2012, the general public could be nominated as torchbearers by others who felt they had made a difference in their local communities. My friend's Mum, Samantha, had nominated me following my Three Peaks Challenge. I was grateful but felt unworthy—many others deserved the honour far more than I, like Becky. But for what it was worth, I was going to milk it with both hands. It was the best recognition I could ever ask for—I almost forgot about everything else. For weeks I visualised that incredible moment, jogging along the road and hoping nobody saw me pretending to hold a giant torch above my head.

A year later I found myself on a train to Scotland, where a stocky, wiry-haired chap from Inverness sat opposite me, and we got on chatting. While sharing stories of our ambitions and his time in the armed forces, he laughed to himself in his hoarse accent.

"Aye..." he began. "If yer' wanna climb Everest, kid, then yer' better stay away from women."

My stammer left me unable to ask his name, too scared to risk embarrassing myself. Not being able to say "hello" or "thank you" was infuriating. But his words certainly never left me—I just wished I'd had them a couple of years earlier. Dealing with teenage girls was, however, good mental preparation for Everest all the same.

In two years my life had changed beyond my imagination, thanks to my challenges, fundraising, and the people I met along the way. Not knowing what would cross my path next was deeply satisfying. I realised that the possibilities were endless.

CHAPTER 8

Indelible Fire

"We cannot hold a torch to light another's path without brightening our own."—Ben Sweetland

A marshal nervously handed me a Mars bar. For thirty-seven minutes or so I'd raced to puke-point. My legs trembled as I ran in vomit-covered shoes past cringing on-lookers at the finish line, including Dad and my stepmum Debbie. I'd finished second place out of nearly six hundred in the Tatton Park ten-kilometre run.

I was just ten seconds short from receiving first place, but it was my best performance to date. I had conquered my two left feet in sports during my school years, and excusing myself from a geography field trip to enter this race had paid dividends.

My new friends at the running club had christened me "The Duck Man" due to my unusual running stride, and it stuck like a tacky theme tune. It was even printed on my club vest, which mortified other runners when I passed them during races. I entered race after race, addicted to the thrill of competition, and was no longer content with doing things just for the fun of it. Competing internationally soon became another pipeline dream. I could never compete on Everest;

reaching the summit was enough, but with running, I always raced to win.

In general, life was better than I had ever known. My anxiety had seemed to crawl under the carpet, and I hoped it would stay there. The hype around the Torch Relay worked wonders for my confidence. I hadn't foreseen that there would be much more on my plate than a three-hundred-metre stretch.

The media was buzzing and I could barely keep up. There was a Torchbearers Ball, and I even had an autograph request from the Philippines (which on reflection was probably some foreign money laundering scam). Mum and I went to a photo shoot in London with the rapper Dizzee Rascal to promote Coca-Cola's sponsorship of the Torch Relay. Seeing myself on thirty-foot billboards in a tacky white tracksuit imitating the Village People was downright weird. Mum came up with the idea that Coca-Cola could sponsor my future Everest climb, and with her tenacious sales skills, wasted no time in sidling up to the manager on the shoot to sell the idea. I still knew very little about sponsorship at this time, but the thought was exciting. Sadly, there is much more to it than meets the eye.

The Future Flames, as we were dubbed, met and shared our stories on a special Facebook forum. I made fantastic friends who shared my beliefs, and a few die-hard "Torchies" still remain close friends today. Meeting them, hearing their stories, and being part of the whole experience was a huge privilege. Amongst them were serial fundraisers, multi-marathoners, dedicated volunteers, athletes, and plenty of humbling journeys. They had become like family in every way. I couldn't contain my enthusiasm, and I remember being told I was obsessed. That was nothing new. This opportunity would be truly once-in-a-lifetime.

On 29th May 2012, day eighteen of the Olympic Torch Relay had finally arrived. I woke with butterflies in my stomach before heading to the meeting point as the flame made its way from Beaumaris to Chester. Earlier that day, the torch would ascend Snowdon with one of my newfound Everest heroes, Sir Chris Bonington. This would be one of the best days of my life, but for my family it became one of the worst.

My Aunt Julie had lost her fight to a terminal brain tumour just a few days earlier. She'd beaten breast cancer, but it came back with a vengeance. Gran was bitter and angry. Granddad was lost. Why had their daughter suffered so much? Mum had always been a caring and thoughtful person, but this knocked her into a shell. They were helpless to watch as she took her last breaths. She was only fifty-two years old. No family should have to go through that, and especially not mine. It hurt our hearts that she couldn't be there just a few days longer to share such a special day. We joked that with her renowned sense of humour she would be there in spirit, trying to trip me up, and I took comfort knowing that my torchbearer role had been a welcome distraction from their anguish, a momentary tonic for the pain. Julie was a light in so many lives, and her charisma and warm heart would be carried within the flame.

On the official relay bus, the seventeen Chester torchbearers were dropped at allocated stretches by the numbered stickers on our outfits. The crowds swarmed the sunny streets outside as we waved back. In front of me was Olympic gymnast Beth Tweddle, and behind, a Russian Gold Medallist swimmer. Being there was beyond my wildest dreams.

I was called forward and handed my torch. At eighty centimetres long, with three sides and eight thousand holes, I laughed to think this giant golden cheese grater was an iconic piece of history.

Crowds swarmed me for photos from the moment I stepped onto the street in Handbridge, Chester, right up until the convoy of vehicles hurtled down the road fifteen minutes later. My legs felt heavy. Simon, the previous runner, appeared around the corner, but I heard the crowd roaring first. I was more fixated on the thing he held above his head: the Olympic Flame.

The Metropolitan police officer dragged me away from the crowd to perform the "torch kiss"—releasing the gas valve on my torch, then bonding the two together to pass the flame on, and I began to weaken in the knees. The crowd fell silent.

"This is your moment to shine," he said, gesturing his hand towards my runway.

I looked ahead nervously. "And for the love of Mr. Bean," I thought, "don't flipping drop it."

Thrusting the ignited torch into the air delighted the crowd, and I took off, cheers roaring in my wake. As I crossed the bridge over the River Dee into the city of Chester, I gazed up at the flames dancing above me. It was the most beautiful thing I had ever seen. I took a moment to reflect on everything—the crippling anxiety, the panic attacks, the low self-confidence, the frustrated, stammer-induced tears, and the countless times I'd felt worthless. They were nowhere to be seen now.

Six members of the police escort ran around me, with officials and camera crews rounding us up like collie dogs.

The closest thing to the top of the world.

My smile could have burst. Waiting at the end of the bridge were several hundred, maybe thousands of people, cameras flashing like lightning. Many had been awaiting my arrival for hours, or more likely, awaiting the flame inches above my head.

"Wow!" I said in disbelief. A line of blokes in full Roman soldier attire stood at the edge of the road stamping their feet and blowing horns. All eyes were on me, and regrettably, I was too shy to do something crowd-pleasing. I'd lost all perception of time and of the world. I could have been on the moon for all I cared.

Dad, family, and friends blended into a sea of beaming faces. Gran looked like she would be crushed, waving a little Union Jack as arms jostled to get photos. My name came from all directions, around and above from the city walls. Awestruck children flapped flags in my path. It seemed my whole village was there.

"Come on, Duck Man!" cheered my friend James from the running club.

Then the horns and whistles faded away. My stretch had come to an abrupt end, before I had a chance to realise it had started. Mum and Gran stood out amongst the sea of happy faces near the finish. I wish I'd gone over to give them a big hug, but railings and my police escort kept me well away—they had previously tackled enthusiastic parents who'd gotten too close to the torchbearer.

After the flame was relayed to the next runner, mine was extinguished and I was whisked away onto the relay bus. We were lost for words, the noise still humming in our ears. Our torches were decommissioned before being returned to us. An unbelievable welcome at the Chester racecourse took me by surprise. The atmosphere was electrifying. I was then dragged towards some BBC cameras for a news interview, speaking live to half a million people, and for the first time, unafraid. Smiling, I stood whilst the camera panned away to the weather reporter beside me. When I watched this later on at home I saw the presenter's arm dragging me, entirely oblivious, out of the frame. It still makes me cringe.

All night the torchbearers were mobbed for even more photos. I'd never thought people could be so attracted to a shiny piece of metal, but they wanted to hold it and touch it as if it were a magic lamp. Finally the evening ended with an incredible firework show and we walked home through the city centre. I felt as burnt out as the torch. Contrary to the famous words of Kurt Cobain, I wasn't sure if it really was better to burn out than fade away; I'd wanted this day to last forever.

The next morning, I cycled to town to watch the torch move onward. I realised how lucky I'd been to run when I did—The Groves and Old Dee Bridge were deserted besides a few ducks quarrelling on the river. I still couldn't make sense of the night before—on three hours of sleep, it all seemed like a fantastic dream. Now when I visit the spot to reminisce, I feel a little sad, but I will always be grateful, and nothing can take those memories away.

CHAPTER 9

Stepping Stones

"Setting goals is the first step in turning the invisible into the visible."—Tony Robbins

Running with the torch was a once-in-a-lifetime experience, and no words could do justice to the experience. I criticized myself harder than ever over my regrets and imperfections. But how could I have prepared for just three hundred metres? There was no practice run or second take. Before I could beat myself up too much, the experience was long over.

Every day I watched the BBC Torch Cam online to follow the torch on its current leg of the relay, sharing the excitement with my new friends as they waited for their turn to run. I cycled everywhere with my torch protruding through the lid of my rucksack. The torch was a great fundraising tool at fairs, schools, clubs, and events. Local kids even started knocking on the front door to see it.

A few months later I went to an exhibit where people were queuing up and paying for a photo with one of the relay torches. Just a week earlier, a couple of unsentimental torchbearers had posted theirs on eBay, some attracting over 150,000 pounds. It would have been an easy ticket to Everest, but integrity was worth more to me.

I inevitably overlooked my A-level exams. The torch alienated me at school, but the positive responses I received from across the country, including attention from radio and news stations, made me proud to be British. This coverage would later help me find sponsorship. First, my former primary asked me to come and speak to the kids about being a torchbearer. Public speaking was a nightmare to me, considering I had missed school on a number of occasions to avoid speaking in front of the class, but I trusted my gut feeling and agreed.

Standing in my torchbearer uniform with over two hundred kids peering up at me—my first ever motivational talk—was terrifying. My heart palpitated, my legs went weak, and I felt awful. But to my amazement, the rest came naturally—not only could I do it, but my passion made me almost entirely fluent. Afterwards I felt confident and accomplished, and missing other opportunities scared me. I started emailing other local schools to offer my speaking services. Public speaking was like climbing. It wasn't just the thrill of being out on the rock or mountain, but the feeling of disproving my limitations. One day in a local shop a woman tapped me on the shoulder to say that, since my talk, her young son had been running around the garden with a coat hanger above his head, "pretending to be Alex." It made me see myself in a new way, to the point that I had to look in the mirror and remind myself who I was.

Mum had asked me whether I would consider making my Mont Blanc climb sponsored for a cancer charity. She was still reeling over losing her only sister, something I could never imagine. Initially I only wanted to support wildlife conservation, but after watching my family's grief, I couldn't say no. I pledged to try and raise one thousand pounds in my Aunt Julie's memory and support REACT for endangered animals at the same time. Most of this money came from a fundraising evening we held for nearly one hundred people. Finding raffle donations from local businesses was long and time consuming. We spent countless hours securing over thirty auction prizes including an Audi sports car for the day, a day of free labour from me and my friend James, and a signed photo by Olympian Jessica Ennis that I was desperate to keep. Thanks to the generosity of many I had raised over six thousand pounds by the end of summer, which made everything worthwhile.

So much was going on at the time that I hardly noticed my worsening running injury. It had gotten so bad that I'd stopped running completely, and none of the physiotherapists I visited could give me answers. In the early stages, walking was still bearable, but I'd lost a considerable amount of fitness from minimal training. I worried how this might affect my performance on Mont Blanc. Come hell or high water, there was no way I would cancel.

At the end of July, I arrived at Chamonix on the border of the French Alps. It was easy to see how the town was a haven for outdoors lovers and adventurers. The forests and alpine peaks were like nothing I had seen before.

Our team of seven was led by Major Phil Ashby, a hardened guide of looming build and stern complexion, with over one hundred ascents of Mont Blanc in his repertoire. We were definitely in good hands. The process of acclimatising and learning glacier skills was new to me, but I quickly learnt the tricks. We spent our first night at the Albert Premier Refuge at 2,702 metres altitude. I woke up at 4:00 a.m. for breakfast feeling fresh whilst everyone else had throbbing headaches, either from the altitude or the Germans snoring in the crowded dormitories. I couldn't get carried away, though—by the next breakfast, even lifting my spoon would be laborious.

Despite being far away from comfort, I felt at home and in my element. My focus had even impressed me. I relished every moment, like abseiling down slopes and reaching the summit of the Petite Fourche under brilliant blue skies I felt I could touch. On the Le Tour glacier we dabbled in crampon techniques, including traversing a slope un-roped above a glacial pond. We retreated to Chamonix to rest before the big push. The weather was kind to us, but a week later we faced huge thunderstorms. Moving up to the Tete Rousse Hut the next morning was tiring, but we made it in good time. The rest of the group with the four other guides would move on to reach the Gouter Hut. I camped outside the Tete Rousse Hut with Phil and a student from Newcastle named Harry due to limited space. As I glanced at the gnarly, imposing rampart of rock ahead of us, and the Gouter Hut perched at the top, I was quite glad at the prospect.

That night, Phil shook the contents of my over-sized rucksack onto the snow.

"What in the bloody hell have you brought that for?" he asked.

The first rule of alpinism was to pack very light. I was learning fast.

Harry and I were crammed into a tent and then awoken at midnight. The black sky twinkled with stars, uninterrupted but for the silhouette of the rock and a small yellow light from the hut window.

We would first cross the Grand Couloir, affectionately known as "death valley," where rock fall had taken many lives. I felt terrible in the unfamiliar altitude. Moving up the rugged jumble of rocks and negotiating the ladders and handrails sent a chill through your gloves. I was now envious of the others who'd had a head-start of two hours, about seven hundred metres' ascent, at least until we all convened at the Gouter Hut for breakfast. The toast was stale, the coffee tasted like liquid mud (so I imagined), and I probably could've slept better on the tarmac of London Heathrow Airport. I was glad to leave at 2:30 a.m. We roped together and moved into the darkness. My head began to pound. I whimpered and moaned at the toll on my oxygen-deprived body. Phil didn't hang around.

"Stop being a big girl!" he barked.

I bit my lip as we plodded on, stepping over a couple patches of orange vomit. There's something liberating about moving into the darkness, ice crunching beneath your feet with only the beam of a head torch to guide you. The rest of the world melts away. I almost fell into a trance. But by the Vallot Refuge I hurt, and by the Bosses Ridge, I was suffering. The humps of the Petite Bosse and the Grande Bosse took the life out of me. I reached into my pocket for an energy bar—I was going to need it—but it had frozen solid. I could barely register anybody around me.

"Can we just stop for ten minutes?" I begged.

"You can stop for ten seconds," Phil said.

The sunrise was a gradient of tangerine hues, illuminating the twisting convexes and delicate seracs. It was a welcome distraction from the feeling of hot lead being poured into my legs and chest. As I looked behind, I realised we were leading an army of head torches, and I was not the only one with a mission. The silhouette of the mountain became clear against the purple skies. My eyes could not absorb it all. In mountains, things can appear much further away than they really are.

I forgot the pain for the final minutes, focusing on my footsteps along the narrow and perilously steep snow arête, with a few thousand foot drop to the left and right. I also forgot about my injury for the first time in months. At about 6:00 a.m., Phil congratulated me as we took our final steps onto the summit of Mont Blanc.

I was standing on the highest peak in the Alps, at 4,810 metres, but I felt as if I was on top of the world. There was no cheering or punching the air; when a moment like that comes, you're too tired to disturb the tranquillity. Seconds later, as if rehearsed, the sunrise bloomed in the sky. The icy air caught in my throat. It was perfect. I shook Phil's hand. Tears welled in my eyes as I rang home whilst Phil tried to get his circulation back.

We only had to share the precipitous seventh heaven platform with three others thanks to Phil's insistence on speed. I put on a full-length orangutan costume I'd carried in my rucksack. I'd sprouted this wacky idea as part of my fundraising for REACT to raise awareness for the plight of

*On the highest peak in the Alps. The sky was the
limit, at least for now.*

the animals. Phil took a photo and we headed down. The strength came back into my legs. It was another step towards Everest in the bag, and I couldn't wait to see where life might take me next.

There was minimal media interest back home, so the idea fell flat, although the director of REACT nicknamed me "Oranguman" from then on. It remains to this day, however, the craziest thing I have ever done, and I don't regret a thing. There are too many people in the world to be normal. In fact, the world would become a pretty boring place if everyone was normal. But heck, what does *normal* even mean? We are all born unique, and if we keep trying to be a copy of someone else, we may never find our own potential.

CHAPTER 10

---◆---

Going Under

"Never give up on something you can't go a day without thinking about."—Winston Churchill

Although I soon dropped my A-levels in mathematics and physics, I did take away one lesson: what goes up must come down again.

Life crashed back to normal. My year of opportunity and excitement had dwindled to disinterest. Nobody gave a toss about a shiny golden stick anymore. I couldn't expect to bask in the glory of being a torchbearer forever, and if I was to be worthy of the honour, then I had to continue what I'd been nominated for. Now that I'd conquered Mont Blanc and my charity fundraising was through, my energy had to be channelled elsewhere. But where? My chronic sore shins were no closer to being healed, and my patience thinned.

Medical professionals across the county, from podiatrists to osteopaths, had recommended just about everything, including giving up on running. One clueless general practitioner even suggested I take up fell running instead.

Soon I was walking down Liverpool Road to the Countess of Chester hospital every week. I had every appropriate test, from blood tests to MRI scans, yet all the professionals had discovered was a possible mature stress fracture. They diagnosed it as shin splints, something that logically couldn't have persisted half as long or stabbed below my knees as I walked the dogs every night. Only copious amounts of ibuprofen and icing my shins every hour brought relief. Every minute I spent on my feet washing neighbours' cars ached and took me backwards from recovery, but Mont Blanc had decimated my bank balance, and washing dishes all weekend barely covered the mounting physiotherapy bills. Swimming, which I hated, maintained my fitness until I injured my lower back and took a complete rest from all training. My intermittent soreness was inconvenient, but being unable to train until pain-free made up for it. It bent me out of the shape I'd only just started to like.

My torchbearer friends had given the distraction and emotional support I'd needed for months. One friend, Ron, was one of the few who could tolerate my frustration, as both of his daughters were athletes. But as the dust gathered on my torch, this relationship began to crumble too.

Being unable to count my blessings made me feel guilty. People around the world faced such hardship, like my aunt had, yet I was fretting at being unable to put one foot in front of the other. Even so, I thought I could no longer serve my purpose if I couldn't be active. My journey to Everest was the only thing that could save me from my demons—I couldn't just stop. As my list of achievements grew, my self-esteem did not, and I felt I needed to tackle bigger and bigger obstacles to prove myself, creating a vicious cycle in which I always needed another goal to affirm my meaning in life.

I crashed back to rock bottom, but this time without a coping mechanism. Playing my guitar, taking photos, or any of my usual hobbies couldn't stop the black hole of depression. Perhaps it had only been subdued by the excitement of the Olympics and Mont Blanc, but now it was out of my control. All the days merged into one. I felt no joy waking up each morning. I closed the door on friends and family when I was told to "grow up." One of the most frustrating parts of depression is being told such a thing, because depression prevents you from doing the things you need to do to help yourself. We can all build mountains from molehills, but chemical imbalances in the brain are very real. Mental strength is fickle. The tenacity required to climb mountains was far different from that required to manage my mental health. At least this time I had the experience to stand and fight it. From previous experience, I knew the NHS mental health department was inadequate and over-subscribed, and I wanted to deal with it myself like last time so help would be available to people who really had no way out themselves. Depression still remains as one of the biggest challenges I have ever faced.

I decided that whilst I couldn't run, I'd work on my nutrition and conditioning so that I could return to my peak faster and keep my running goals within reach. Instead of A-level textbooks, my head was buried in sports science books, but the more I learnt, the worse my health grew. I tried to restrict various food groups like wheat, dairy, red meat, sugar, and fried foods to achieve the perfect athlete diet. Amongst many other fads, I tried twenty-four-hour fasting, where I would consume only black coffee in order to reduce my body fat and chance of lifestyle diseases. Living like some devout hippie had become the only challenge I could find, but adhering to the many rules of this bohemian regime led to a vicious cycle of continual relapse: stuffing myself until I felt sick and guilty, thus reinforcing my feelings of inferiority. I probably had issues with food because of the three seizures I'd had during meals as a child. Even though my appetite was ravenous, I would count the grams of fat in a biscuit, convinced it would induce a heart attack.

Food was now the only pleasure left in my life. Scientific studies on mice have shown that sugar is more addictive than cocaine, so making desserts in the kitchen at work was far from helpful. Food only bottled my frustration, and one night I broke down and stormed out, sobbing uncontrollably. Usually I would walk home at 10:30 p.m. in the gloom listening to "February Stars" by the Foo Fighters. The melancholy lyrics suited my mood. My dogs Harley and Hooch would come greet me as I slumped onto the kitchen floor and clung tearfully to their scraggy fur. It was the best comfort I got.

Mental health problems and disordered eating, however you gloss them up, are nothing to be ashamed of. They are neither a choice nor sign of weakness. I share this to provide hope to others who feel alone like nobody understands, because if it wasn't for the love of my family, I don't know what I would have done next.

I know how much a book can help someone in a time of crisis. One day I went to visit my grandma Betty in Sheffield where Dad had grown up. The train journey home was miserable and made worse by the carriage of drunken football supporters.

Summoning the motivation to do anything was a challenge. My friend Rich recommended I read *Mud, Sweat, and Tears* by the adventurer Bear Grylls, and I would soon be indebted to him. Books had never interested me much, but the story of Bear's parachuting accident and his near-paralysation hooked me. His own hopes of reaching the summit of Everest had been crushed like the three vertebrae in his back, but after intensive physiotherapy, he recovered to reach the summit just eighteen months later, aged twenty-three.

As I gazed into the wet winter blackness of the train carriage window I smiled my biggest smile since Mont Blanc. The weight of the world had been lifted from my shoulders.

I wasn't an SAS reservist, nor had I endured one of the most torturous military selection processes in the world; I was an ambitious teenager with a pair of gammy legs. But I felt that if Bear could succeed with the right mindset, then I could, too. I had just needed a new focus. Reading Bear's book had re-instilled my belief that I had to continue pursuing my dream no matter how big the risk.

Sometimes we can pinpoint pivotal moments. Sometimes they remain unseen. A couple of days later, I remember sitting on the sofa in our living room with the dogs snoring beside me. Harley would occasionally get a bad dream and boot my computer from my lap. While browsing the web for inspiration, I found a striking photo of Mount Everest. Goosebumps prickled up my arms as I remembered the sheer, raw joy of gasping for air at the top of a mountain. Feeling alive. Everest was the limit of human endurance.

Everest had crossed my mind every day since my first rock climb. My research revealed that climbing Everest in 2014 would make me the youngest Briton to scale Everest via the Southeast Ridge route in Nepal. This was a loose record, as the current record holder, George Atkinson, had been sixteen when he climbed via the north side, but it was enough of a selling point to market myself and find sponsorship. This was my chance. I didn't care whether I was the youngest, fastest, or the first to play the violin in a chicken costume on the summit. It was never about breaking records, but making the best of what I had. I decided 2014 would be the year that I would climb Mount Everest. After all, a goal is a dream with a deadline.

Like Bear, I wouldn't change my plans because of the injury. I'd work that part out later. I thought corporate sponsorship was my best chance, and the older I was, the harder it would be. Later I learned otherwise, but I made the decision with the best information that I had available at the time. Some climbers had described sponsorship as a form of natural selection harder than the climb itself; you would only succeed if you wanted it enough, and even then, there was no guarantee. It was a bold ask. Actually, it was bloody enormous, verging on insanity. I'd given myself less than eighteen months to prepare and fundraise over forty thousand pounds. I had to act before life got in the way. The scale of the challenge only enticed me more. By now I'd gained a good understanding of what Everest required by learning from those who'd already been there. Now it was time to do it myself.

I was unable to sleep until early morning with the plans blossoming in my mind. I felt alive for the first time in months. I'd have to hang on tight—it was going to be a bumpy ride, but one day, I really would live the dream.

PART 3

LONG & WINDING ROAD

CHAPTER 11

Aut Viam Inveniam
Aut Faciam

"The difference between the impossible and the possible is merely a measure of man's determination."—Captain James Thain

A spot on the two-month Everest expedition with Tim Mosedale would cost about 35,000 pounds. Tim would take care of the logistics and lead us on the mountain, and the rest covered my flights, mountain permits, kit, food, staff, oxygen, and everything else. Whilst I was grateful for my parents' support, they weren't going to sign me a cheque. Dad worked in London as a technical manager for a lighting company, whilst Mum and my stepdad worked hard with their successful taxi business. It took a long time for both to come round. Dad said it was a lot of money to spend on a holiday. Mum had demanded that I stop fundraising until my A-level exams were finished, which I ignored.

I guess they thought I should be responsible, especially once I turned eighteen. But the responsibility of making my dream happen was in my hands and mine alone. I'd been brought up to work hard, and I had nobody else to blame if I didn't make it.

An orthopaedic consultant I met on New Year's Eve 2012 suggested I might never be able to return to proper training, especially not in time to climb the world's highest mountain. I was still without a diagnosis and my level of the stress hormone cortisol was also very low. I just had to believe it would sort itself out in time, as I had already got started. Accepting that my fitness was long gone, I allowed myself to indulge at Christmas before the chaos began.

"Why the rush?" was the first thing people asked.

"Because it's there," would have sounded pretentious.

"Oh, you mean Everest Base Camp?" they would say. The frequency of this assumption made me embarrassed to bring it up in conversation.

One friend asked me if I achieved my life ambition so young, what would I possibly do afterwards? I said that reaching the summit at any age was an incredible achievement, but doing it as a teenager would show other young people what they were capable of. The problem, as such, was that once I committed myself to something, I refused to back down. This decision would make or break me. Giving in to my weaknesses was a one-way ticket back to the pit of depression.

Depression never completely goes away. Committing to a new cause helped me regain confidence, but my antidote had also become the problem. When I didn't have that feeling of achievement I was ripped to shreds. I still hadn't figured out the cause of my depression. I had just accepted the cycle and gotten used to working through the bad days.

Getting to Everest would require planning skills, clear thinking, and the ability to delegate. I had none of those. I wasn't creative, so I usually let others do the thinking, then helped develop the ideas. The only examples I had were the others who had found sponsorship, like Becky, Matt, and Mollie, as well as James Ketchell, Bonita Norris, and Rhys Jones, who gave me heaps of advice. I compiled it all and analysed how they had gone about sponsorship to sketch out an action plan. The sponsorship market was always evolving, and many others were on the same quest. Remembering their dedication kept me going in the hardest times. I even wrote a quote Becky had mentioned, "The greatest suffering brings the greatest successes," across my bedroom wall.

Earlier in the summer I had received an email from a man named Chris Spray with an idea for charity fundraising. I didn't understand the concept and nearly dismissed it, but decided to hear him out. Chris was short, stocky, and had a friendly face. He greeted me and handed me a plastic tub of a stodgy, pale mixture which he introduced as "Kelly the friendship cake." The mixture would expand over a period of ten days, and each batch would produce four cakes you could pass onto friends and continue the cycle. After this, you would add fruit before baking. Each cake mix came with a small donation card. It wasn't a great success and I ate most of it once I'd run out of neighbours, but Kelly had a trick up her sleeve. I found out that Chris also practiced Neuro-Linguistic Programming, a subjective study of how people excel. Similar to coaching, NLP studies aspects of our thoughts like positivity and self-doubt. Understanding how and why we feel certain ways can help us to change our thought processes. I got in touch with Chris again to ask whether he might be able to help my stammer. I feared that otherwise, sponsors might never take me seriously.

I met him at his house one November evening for a chat. I'd been referred a number of times for speech therapy, but the appointments took months to arrive and I gave up hope that it would work. I never thought of myself as disabled, but as much as my parents reassured me it didn't matter, it still frustrated me. Chris told me the stammer was from subconscious thoughts and emotional triggers deep in my past, and was actually a form of self-preservation. The stammer was caused by miniature anxiety attacks in my vocal muscles. When I thought about trying to stop the stammer, the muscles would seize up.

Before I left, I confided to Chris, "I really want to make a difference in the world. My goal is to climb Everest, but I don't have a clue how I'll get there. What do you think?"

Chris thought for a moment. He had a sparkle in his eyes. "I don't think you need to know all the steps," he said. "You just have to start, and find the way."

I was eager to know more. Hearing somebody else speak so positively was what I really needed.

"I just don't think I'll do it by washing dishes on four pounds an hour," I said.

He agreed, then asked how many Facebook friends I had. I tallied it up but didn't understand.

He smiled. "35,000 pounds? You know, that's just each one of your friends giving you about thirty pounds each."

"Do you think anybody would sponsor me?" I asked.

"Yes. It's a great story! I can see it being a documentary or book one day."

Chris's perspective helped me see the possibilities I had missed. I wrote everything down when I got home. I had to start believing in myself, and before I could put unhelpful excuses or negative thoughts in my mind, Chris would cut me off. He took great satisfaction in understanding people, helping them to be fully themselves and watching them grow. He was self-assured, a practicing Christian, and the sort of person who would share his last meal with you even if you didn't deserve it. I discovered he had led operations in some of the largest FMCG businesses across Europe and had a wealth of experience that I could tap into, right when I needed corporate sponsorship. When I could have backed away from the challenge, he became my mentor and coach. Coaching is about questions rather than answers. Mentoring isn't mollycoddling; it's pointing the way and providing the inspiration throughout peaks and pitfalls. Chris believed in me from the word go, and that meant the world to me.

My first step was to produce a sponsorship proposal, a bit like a holiday brochure, selling what I was doing, how much I needed, and what the sponsors would get in return. I worked on it until it looked first-rate. Businesspeople were busy; I'd be lucky if they didn't delete my email, which they surely would do if it didn't grab their attention. I had no marketing experience, but for everything I didn't know, I found someone who did. A fellow torchbearer had worked in sponsorship marketing and kindly gave her time to listen to my questions over coffee. One of the best bits of advice I got was to "GET THEIR BLOODY ATTENTION." See what I did there? One adventurer told me to take up golf—but wearing stripy trousers was a step too far. A famous polar explorer told me not to even bother trying, which spurred me on even more. There really is nothing better than doing what people say you cannot do.

Besides the adversity, I needed something different to sell. I brought my notepad everywhere and brainstormed ideas on paper, even sticking post-it notes to the Everest poster in my room. The Olympic torch seemed promising. The Chinese had already taken a lit torch to the top of Everest in the 2008 Olympic Games, but mine could still help me get noticed. I was also endorsed by renowned explorers Sir Chris Bonington and Sir Ranulph Fiennes. Eventually, I came up with the slogan "Climb4Change," which aimed to change the way young people followed the path instead of achieving their potential.

Chris also pointed me towards the right places to find the right people and raise awareness of what I was doing. It was not what I knew, but who I knew. As a result, one of the first to contact me out of the blue was Paul White from Plymouth, a financial and adventure sports consultant. He knew his stuff, having worked with the likes of Formula One driver Mark Webber, and now wanted to focus his efforts on helping young people. He offered his expertise to help me reach my goal, specifically to take care of sponsorship so I could focus on preparation. I was grateful, but decided I wanted to do it myself; this was my chance to earn it and see what I could do. In his thirty years of experience, I had been the only person to refuse his help. To my relief, Paul deeply respected my drive, and has been a friend ever since.

As if raising the money wasn't demanding enough, Everest was no playground. It had broken some of the hardest mountaineers on the planet. Tim Mosedale had high standards for his team, and that was the team I wanted to be part of. Not everyone had the time to build up a comprehensive mountaineering CV before they decided to aim for the highest. I would have to compress several years worth of training into eighteen months. There was lots to be done. But I pledged to do whatever it took to know my stuff once I got to the slopes.

Baruntse, a remote and beautiful 7,129 metre peak in the Himalayas of Nepal, became my first objective. It had serious altitude, low technicality, and smaller overheads than an eight-thousand-metre peak. A British expedition company called Adventure Peaks was putting together a guided expedition to climb Baruntse the following autumn. They were happy to take me, providing I completed a Scottish winter mountaineering training course beforehand. Without hesitation, I pulled a sick note out of sixth form and made the trip alone to Onich in the western highlands of Scotland.

My technical skills were way off the mark and I knew it. Mountaineering didn't come naturally to me. Fortunately, we had a long and fierce winter, and I could practice my ice axe self-arrests down slopes in local fields where nobody else could see me. But all my preparation hung in the balance of a revered sports physiotherapist named Andy Hall. He was my last resort. I followed his intensive programme of flexibility, rehabilitation, and conditioning exercises for nearly an hour each day, and miraculously, my condition began to lessen after fifteen months. I was able to start cycling again. Another bone scan showed that there was nothing wrong. The consultant could not explain my chronic pain. The only possible cause was a sudden growth spurt in my tibia bones that inflamed the muscle ligaments as they pulled on the fascia where they attached.

"Hang on... so you're saying I actually *could have* continued training without doing any damage?" I asked. He nodded.

Growing pains. I'd heard it all. They were soon to be the least of my concerns. After putting myself through all of this, I thought, Everest had better be worth the effort.

CHAPTER 12

Rejections

"Success consists of going from failure to failure without loss of enthusiasm."—*Winston Churchill*

By May, I had started running again. I had to be disciplined, although I was always tempted to speed up when running past girls. My ultra-runner friend Jon shook my hand after a two-mile trail run, the furthest I'd ran in eighteen months. I was just grateful to be back in the outdoors, and I'd been discharged from the hospital only nine weeks before the trip. I still worried whether I would be strong enough for Baruntse. It was a good thing I still had a strong heart, because my body would soon be working overtime.

I had to raise an extra seven thousand pounds for Baruntse in six months. My teachers worried that too many extra-curricular activities would make me neglect my future, but I put my backside on the line and swore I could pull it off. Everest would be an investment in my future; and indeed, it taught me bigger life lessons than school ever did. They kindly gave me special permission to hold a non-uniform day and cake sales, which raised thousands of pounds.

There was a catch—I had to give an assembly about my plans. I was petrified. If my body wasn't so knackered, I'd have struggled to sleep all weekend. When I stood up that week in front of the other students, my confidence kept the stammer away. The teachers at my school were supportive of my challenges and fundraising, most of all the head teachers' assistant, Pam. She put me in touch with a local businessman who donated two thousand pounds towards Everest from his own pocket because his business couldn't sponsor me. Pam also told my story to acclaimed author Jeffrey Archer, who donated handsomely. It was never about standing around rattling a bucket, though. "Donation" suggests that the donor gets nothing in return; sponsorship is very different. But when anyone made donations simply because they wanted to help, their generosity blew me away.

I scheduled another fundraising night at my local golf club. I'd been invited to the golf club previously to meet Olympic rower Sir Steve Redgrave to get items signed for my auction. I was so star-struck, I missed the chance to ask him for an endorsement, asking instead whether my Olympic running ambitions were realistic. He said "never say never," although I knew I couldn't. Being a professional athlete didn't matter to me anymore, only Everest.

The night finally came. A local band donated their services and through hundreds of emails I had received signed items from celebrities to auction. One of my colleagues even offered his time to cook a three-course meal as a raffle prize. Even though I'd spent hours knocking on doors and selling tickets, barely anybody showed up for the first hour. By the end of the night, however, I'd raised another three thousand pounds, and celebrated with horrendous dad-style dancing.

I then won a grant from a charitable trust and received sponsorship from a solicitor and his business partner. Baruntse was in the bag, but I had barely scratched the surface for Everest.

When I first sent my sponsorship proposal to Chris Spray, I expected it to be binned. My perfectionism was my biggest enemy and the year was slipping away fast. Chris told me it was exceptional and to get on with it. With me it could never be that straightforward, of course, and he patiently listened to my questions several times a week. Rather than giving me the answer, he would ask me questions to help me answer it for myself.

Having two taxi drivers in the family paid dividends. They sang my praises to businessmen, and I gave my proposal to every lead I got. When I heard about businesses who had spent 26,000 pounds on a boardroom table, I hoped they might part with enough to fund my expedition. I offered various tiers of sponsorship to stretch the net. The bigger the investment, the more they would get. I looked for any company that would want to be involved and learnt the tricks to find email addresses in minutes, though they made a valiant effort to hide them from people like me. When no replies came within the first week, I was convinced that my email account was broken. It took a while to understand what was going on at the other end of the line. I was a product, and I needed to trust I was selling myself the right way. Once I did, I had to choose who to approach. I didn't want to be sponsored by cigarette brands or companies destroying the rainforests, and the chances of John's Kebab Shop wanting to take their brand to the top of the world were slim. But I never knew for certain. One mantra that stuck in my mind was, "a shy bairn gets no sweets."

With this in mind, I won the Diana Award for "Courageous Citizen," an award that recognises the power of young people to change the world. When I attended the award ceremony in the Barclays bank headquarters in Canary Wharf, London, I strolled up to one of the most senior directors with one of my homemade business cards. Even Dad was surprised, but I had to do whatever I needed to.

"Have you tried Richard Branson? He's loaded!" people suggested. They don't realise he gets thousands of similar requests every month.

"How about Everest Windows?" was another. Nope, never thought of that one.

Every contact I did make, however, I followed up ruthlessly. Making enquiries on the phone had been the most effective way for the other climbers, but I thought nobody would take me seriously, though at least they might remember me. My cousin Kate followed up a few enquiries by phone, though I did try. Sometimes it took a full day for me to find the courage. One day I got through to a global vice president. Seconds later, Sid, our African grey parrot, shrieked, "Help, they've turned me into a parrot!" in the background, and I had to hang up because of my laughter. It worked in my favour that email was becoming the accepted form of communication.

Every day for a year, I challenged myself to send more emails than the day before. This was not easy with my short attention span. Maybe it was the fear of failure and the time pressure that helped me copy, paste, and prowl the web like a robot. Seventy-five percent of my emails got no response, but I hoped to at least get a "no" so I could move along. Most sent a generic response about their community initiatives, and one grumpy CEO accused me of circulating spam. He was probably just having a bad day at work. One of the earliest businesses I tried said no because it was too dangerous and they were a safety company. The rejections stopped bothering me once I used them to fine-tune my approach. One thing I learnt to stress was my epilepsy. I'd been seizure-free for so long that I wondered whether I was still classified as epileptic, though I occasionally had dizzy episodes of bright vision and ringing in my ears that I never understood, but this was the first concern people had.

The reality was that most businesses were more interested in what I could do for them rather than my dream or the adversity I faced. I had a lot to offer them. My inexperience made me vulnerable to exploitation, but I stood my ground. To protect myself from businessmen, I sort of had to become one. My emails were regularly misunderstood, but many others commented I had an excellent story and an impressive sponsorship proposal. Some seemed genuinely disappointed they didn't have the budget. Getting free items like headphones, gloves, and boxes of cereal bars wasn't quite what I needed, but it was a nice gesture. Finding kit sponsorship, and thus discounted kit, was a bit different. It would reduce the overhead, since some of my equipment cost the same as a small car, but I couldn't accept rubbish gear for the sake of saving money. I was lucky that two of the leading brands came on board quite early, and even luckier when the Craghoppers sales team organised a fancy-dress carwash at their offices to raise money for the expedition.

Finding the motivation wasn't hard. Once I had applied myself one hundred percent, I had everything I needed. I couldn't bear to go to bed each night without feeling satisfied, so I worked until I fell asleep at the keyboard. Absolute dedication came at a cost. If I wouldn't waste time or money, I couldn't expect friends to waste theirs on me, and the ones who waited were worth making time for. Many of the friends who told me I needed to have fun would later ask me how on earth I managed to get so many opportunities. I did what I had to, not what I wanted to do—at least until Hooch barged into the office when it was time for his walk.

Taking the dogs out in the forest was my only real escape and chance to think. There was no point trying to enjoy my hobbies because my conscience said every minute was another sponsor not being approached. Even on the bus or walking the dogs, I sent emails on my phone or wrote in my diary for my future book. Sooner or later, sleep would catch up to me, and I once fell asleep in the bath and ruined my mobile phone. It wasn't much fun, and it didn't involve my passion for the outdoors, but it paid off.

Before Everest, I had plans to be a scuba diving instructor in Australia and travel the world. I'd wanted to volunteer abroad for orangutans too, but before I was old enough to apply, I was embedded in my Everest journey. Once I'd accepted I couldn't do everything, I chose what I felt most important. This was where adventure and achievement diverged. I didn't just want to see and experience the world, or traverse Costa Rica on rollerblades and get some quirky photos. I began calling myself an endurance adventurer because I wanted to complete feats that tested the parameters of my physical and mental endurance and were challenging enough to encourage donations for charity. I stopped calling myself a mountaineer or a climber because mountains just happened to be one of the places that I found my challenge. That doesn't mean I'll hang my boots up after Everest, though.

Sponsorship became my full-time job, but the difference between this and a nine-to-five job was that there was no weekend. Raising money from sponsorship rather than earning it myself was no easier. The hours are much longer, and you don't know if you will get paid at the end of your fifteen-month contract. But picturing the moment of success on Everest each day was enough. Sacrificing everything was easy if I kept the end result in mind. I imagined falling into the snow at the top of the world under the deep purple sky. Would I see the curvature of the earth? What would my first words be? However I planned it in my head, it would be worth it. Until I got there, Everest wasn't making me very happy. Option A was carry on, suffer, and succeed. Option B was quit and suffer. Only one would give me the end result, and only then would I conquer adversity once and for all. I just had to make sure I didn't run out of steam before I reached the station.

Early on, another Everest climber advised me that I was putting out negative vibes on my Twitter account because nobody had replied to my emails. Hearing that sponsors didn't support sympathy changed my attitude. It was only a matter of time before I got the one "yes" I needed. I got my first sponsorship meeting through a tip-off by a friend, and waiting in their office reception was nerve-wracking, especially when minutes beforehand, I dribbled my white chocolate mocha down my business suit.

The marketing manager met the opportunity with enthusiasm.

"I can see the return on investment," he said across the table. "Excellent pitch."

I bounced outside into the car believing it was in the bag, which after three months seemed a bit farfetched. It was. After not responding for months, they got cold feet. Their response stung. You'd think they couldn't say no, considering the company was called "YES."

Through his own network, Chris had introduced me to a huge business he knew well. My sponsorship proposal fought its way up to the vice president, but even with the right people on my side, it was a fragile game. Some rejections lead to bigger opportunities down the line. I had accepted my mission, and I was the only thing standing in my way.

CHAPTER 13

Shy Bairns Get Nowt'

"Working hard for something we don't care about is called stress, working hard for something we love is called passion."—Simon Sinek

Minutes before I left for work one Friday evening, I sent an email to the managing director of Textlocal, a mobile communications firm, and one of the biggest providers of bulk SMS messaging in the UK. I'd never heard of them before, a good reason they'd be interested in sponsorship.

A week later I took a day off school to meet the three directors. For a seventeen-year-old armed only with passion and paperwork, I kept my calm well. One of the first things they asked was whether I was in college. They seemed impressed even though I wasn't. Months later, the managing director emailed me and said they wanted to support me as my first major sponsor. They would invest thousands to get the prized summit shot, positioning, and the major media coverage. I bounded downstairs, hugged the dogs, and skipped around the house. Moments like these made the pitfalls worthwhile.

The delight in Chris's voice on the phone was unmistakable. But this time, I wouldn't count my eggs until they'd hatched. It was an anxious wait. After hearing nothing for months, I left voicemails for all three directors (although it took twenty attempts until I could record one smoothly).

I did everything I could to sway things in my favour. Social media became more important than ever—I couldn't inspire people without telling the story. It brought so much more than I bargained for. I was immersed into a like-minded outdoors community where I felt I belonged, at least to begin with, and it connected me to people like Ste Rumbelow, who was set to trek solo across Mongolia the following year. We got along brilliantly. A few years my elder and from the rural county of Rutland, Ste was athletic and clued up when it came to technology, cycling, and pretty much everything I did. He became my right-hand man and the graphic designer for Climb4Change, plus everything since.

Putting myself in the public eye came at an extra cost. Some trolls said I was on a high horse and even hoped I fell off Everest and died. They had no idea I was my own biggest critic. Leaving them to stew in their mothers' basements, I continued making progress. Dreams do come true, and sceptics hate it.

My peers at school only seemed to care about exam grades and university. Thinking it would be worthwhile at some point, I had applied to study at the University of Cumbria. I was so focused on finding sponsorship, I shoved it to the back of my mind and opted to take a gap year first—a gap year that never really ended.

Lads' holidays, cars, nights out, and designer clothes had no place on my agenda either. Climbing Everest was all that mattered. For the same reasons, at twenty years old, I am still teetotal to alcohol. Witnessing the damage alcohol had caused in my family unnerved me, and I remained resistant to peer pressure until I went to a sixth form party to see if I'd been missing much. The alcohol was rancid, how I'd imagined bleach would taste, and I had a panic attack when I felt I'd lost control. Dodging the piles of vomit, I cycled home satisfied that I'd missed out on absolutely nothing. I was happy being the coffee-flavoured chocolate in the box. I had no desire to fit in.

On A-level exam results day, I scraped the grades required and skipped outside. Having fulfilled my promise, I smiled at the head of my year. I wanted to be remembered for all the right reasons. Leaving sixth form was emotional, but it meant I could spend every hour of the day working on the project without teachers catching me skipping lessons to attend meetings.

"So who are you meeting again?" Mum would ask.

"I've already told you," I would groan.

"There's so many, I've forgotten!"

My sarcastic responses, from the Pope to the Prime Minister, soon stopped her bothering.

Sometimes I didn't know what I was asking for, but opportunities surprised me. I never emailed asking for money, only to meet for coffee. Many agreed to meet and backed out. Some broke the ice more abruptly. One memorably asked, "So how many bodies are there on Everest nowadays?" I took a scary jaunt through Brixton, south London, to meet a charitable foundation for a grant. Over coming months, sponsors of all sizes came on board, and I checked my emails with delight. Each one had the potential to take me to Everest, and opening emails had never been so exciting. Often nothing would come through for a week, then I'd get thirty rejections at once. Negotiating so many partnerships was tough. I had to provide a return and keep everyone happy, though I enjoyed the challenge of being a project manager. The journey felt within the realm of possibility when I signed the major sponsorship contract with Textlocal Ltd. That was the sweet return on investment that I'd needed to continue believing. I was over the moon. I couldn't stop, of course. There were still 15,000 pounds to raise.

When Mum and my stepdad went off on holiday in the summer, I stayed behind. Two weeks were too valuable to lose. Everything I did had to fit the action plan. Whilst they stayed up till the early hours in the Mediterranean, I was working through the night on a presentation for the CEO at a huge corporation. Both my suit and my lateness were unfashionable. The day that trains run on time, the world will know peace. I soon realised I'd forgotten the hard drive with my presentation. In the office, the assistant asked whether I'd brought a laptop. Damn. It could only get better. I composed myself and spoke to them with the courage I'd felt on top of Mont Blanc. It was well received. On the way home that evening I received an email from the CEO:

> *"Whilst I know it will be disappointing, based on where you are today, I cannot justify a sponsorship on either of the above two grounds. However, as what will hopefully be a ray of hope, if you can progress the idea of a documentary to reality then you have your second major sponsor [providing we are one of only two major sponsors]. The challenge is yours."*

I would rise to the challenge. Chris said that was the best email he'd ever seen. I'd been working closely with a Cardiff filmmaker on a documentary about Everest climbers and my story, but it still had to be commissioned by a broadcaster. We sprung to action to approach other filmmakers. If he couldn't produce it, I'd find someone who would. Sadly, it still didn't happen.

Closer to home, it wasn't long before I'd lose even more. I felt a bit of heaven on earth, walking the dogs with Granddad on a summer afternoon, sunlight trickling through the trees and blackberries on the bushes. Hooch chugged up the path but seemed to be struggling. I lifted him into the car. He had his head in the bag of sweets on the dashboard, so perhaps it was a false alarm. Over dinner, I poked fun at my grandparents' tubby old dog, and Granddad told me not to speak ill of the dead. His words would soon haunt me.

Later that night, Hooch kept my feet warm as usual, but something wasn't right. He went limp and slumped onto the floor. I ran upstairs to wake Mum and my stepdad, crying that Hooch was in a bad way. I was back by his side as he struggled for breath, stiffened up, and then shook violently. He wasn't breathing. His eyes were wide and vacant. He let out a horrific groan as his whole body seized. We hurried him into the back of the minibus and raced to the vet. I gave him CPR, but I knew it was too late.

The vet placed his hand on his chest and shook his head. "He's gone. I'm very sorry."

I wailed in disbelief, then fell to quiet shock. Life would never be the same again.

The next day, I broke the news to Dad.

"Hi, Al," he said. "You alright, love?"

I choked back the tears. I'd never heard Dad cry before.

Hooch spent his life at my side, and I was kind of glad he went the same way. My stepdad brought biscuits home for comfort food. It was the first day of the year I hadn't sent an email, but I forced myself on a run in the forest. Bereavement was something I couldn't train for. Hiding my puffy eyes behind sunglasses, I remembered how Hooch used to chase squirrels up trees. We were similar in that way: chasing things we might never catch, but with great enthusiasm. He was always a comedian. He had an innate ability to destroy home DIY projects or give himself zebra stripes from a freshly painted wall left unattended, and you could just tell by his expression that he knew exactly what he was doing.

Shortly beforehand, one of my old school friends had died in a motorbike accident. He was only eighteen. It was a harsh reminder of my own mortality. Everest was selfish and dangerous, I'd always known that, but we are all selfish—it's a human survival mechanism. Going on holiday to lie on beaches and indulging in restaurant food is also selfish, same with smoking, running a marathon, or watching a football match every Saturday instead of spending time with your family. There is nothing heroic about dying on Everest, but doing something else was never really an option. I'd face whatever that path dealt me. Some people might think they're invincible, but I think we have to find the balance of risk and reward rather than fear what may or may not happen. If we take no risks at all, we can't satisfy our potential. I started to believe that if we fear the end before we can see it, we are not living life to our best ability. As the famous poem by Linda Ellis says, "Life is two dates and a dash, and what matters is the dash in between."

CHAPTER 14

Growing Pains

"There is of course never any point in crying over spilt milk—the key is to learn from failures and then to keep going."—Sir Ranulph Fiennes

Seven-thousand-metre peaks are deadly serious. On 12th October 2013, the date had come. I would fly to Nepal for the four-week Baruntse training expedition, a new type of adversity to overcome.

I amused the neighbours by walking Harley in my new Millet eight-thousand-metre expedition boots and spent the night in my giant Marmot sleeping bag to get used to my gear. An easy walk high up on top of Kentmere Horseshoe in the Lake District gave me some confidence, but my shin problems made me paranoid of re-injury, and I'd been over cautious with my training. There was nothing more I could do but trust my determination and give it everything I had.

"This is going to bring opportunities you won't see coming," Chris told me over an early morning coffee. "Go get it."

All afternoon I sent out as many sponsorship emails as I could. My grandparents came round for a farewell lunch at our favourite cafe, the Greedy Pig. My overeating was the least of my priorities, like my most irrational fear: flying. The expedition was far more dangerous, but before watching TV became a luxury, I began watching a series called *Air Crash Investigation*. Like with my injury, too much knowledge became my enemy.

My fears came down to control. During my work experience at school I had flown a Cessna 152 propeller plane under supervision. If we nosedived to the ground, at least it would be at my own admission. In my own hands I felt relaxed. Taking Harley to the vet just two weeks before the trip had put me in the hospital. My vision whirred and my heart raced as the vet spoke in graphic detail. I fell to the floor of the consulting room and got a concussion. As I was wheeled into an ambulance, Harley had sat outside almost shaking his head. Right now, I missed him more than anyone. I knew he might not be there when I got back.

Butterflies fluttered in my stomach as Dad took me to Heathrow Airport to meet my team for the first time. Paul soon arrived, and I looked so misplaced he didn't recognise me at first. He was a forty-something from Sheffield, ex-military, and now a bodyguard who had worked for the British Embassy. He was tough and chiselled but easy to get along with. Francis was our expedition leader, an unassuming bloke in his mid-twenties with a wealth of mountaineering experience. We boarded the flight and I tried to soothe my nerves. I'd beaten the injury, the deepest low in my life. Whether this was all in vain depended on my success on this expedition, but I would just take each day at a time and learn as much as I could.

"Boots off, sir," barked a security guard at Mumbai Airport, pointing at the clunky Millet boots as I tried to explain the only prohibited items were the feet inside. Damn baggage weight allowance. We touched down in Kathmandu, the capital city of Nepal. As we shuttled through the streets, I was surprised at the poverty outside, where stray dogs loitered amongst worn-out buildings. It was humid and dirty, and face masks gave people little protection from the smog. The dilapidated shop fronts left me wondering how on earth these people made enough money to survive. The welcome we received, however, was far less shabby.

Monsoon-like rains hit the city as we explored the streets by night, where we met Phil, the last member of our team. Phil was a slight, easy-going Australian in his late thirties, and incredibly fit. Over dinner it became clear that they were all more experienced than me, each having been to serious altitude before. They seemed to accept my presence, but suggested I might lack the required endurance. The foul weather persevered and shelved our plans to travel to Lukla the following day. We were delayed for a number of days, which we spent exploring the historical sites instead. Our itinerary was becoming compromised, so our agent, Mohan, gave us the option of a helicopter flight into Lukla at the cost of 250 dollars each. We had little choice but to take it.

Tenzing-Hillary Airport is a miniscule mountain airstrip situated in Lukla, a village in the lower Solukhumbu district, the main gateway into the Everest region. At 2,820 metres, it provides extreme challenges, such that only specially trained senior pilots are allowed to fly there. It has been the site of numerous fatal accidents, earning itself a reputation as the world's most dangerous airport. I had read plenty about it. The runway, with its sloping gradient, was steep enough to allow the small propeller planes to gain enough speed to lift off and avoid tumbling down the ravine at the other end. Planes only have one chance to land. There is no go-around with such steep terrain. Brilliant.

"Where's the helicopter?" I asked. There was a beast parked on the tarmac of Kathmandu Tribhuvan Airport.

This wasn't any old helicopter. It was a battered Russian Mi-17 chopper that looked fresh from a war. Paul knew them well from the army.

"These things are good old war horses. Indestructible," he said. "It's probably still got a few bullet holes in it, too!"

I stood aghast in the pouring rain as we were ushered on board my worst nightmare. Paint peeled off the bare panels. The submarine-like windows had been scratched opaque.

Kitbags were piled above our heads down the aisle, trapping us in the disfigured seats, and the machine was obviously overweight. When I thought it couldn't get much worse, our captain clambered aboard, whom I can only describe as the Russian equivalent of Mayor Boris Johnson. His stripy, faded t-shirt did not cover the beer gut spilling over his tracksuit bottoms. Francis confided later on that he'd been very close to taking us all off. The decrepit machine chugged to life with a deafening hum and lifted off the ground towards our fate. Surely there were more constructive ways to kill myself for 250 dollars, I thought. When we finally touched down, I could open my eyes again. I had at least conquered my fear of flying.

At Lukla we met our team. We had two climbing Sherpas: Ongchhu and Phur Temba, who had climbed Baruntse five times. A younger, curly-haired man called Thoman was our sirdar, the expedition manager. The cook, Purna, was a cheerful, greying man who could only say "thank you, sir" in English. We had several porters too, and it made me sad that they were treated like underdogs when they were doing the hardest work of all by heaving our supplies to the destination each day.

We began the expedition by trekking in the lower foothills, gradually moving higher to acclimatise our bodies. We hiked against a backdrop of lush alpine greenery, waterfalls, and humid, forested valleys. Curious locals watched us passing through their villages, moving further away from civilisation into an entirely subsistent way of life. Inquisitive children would chirp "namaste!" and follow me for a closer look at my iPhone. We were always welcomed warmly, despite the occasional altitude headache.

The tranquil foothills merged into foggy passes and pathless moraine as we pushed towards the snow line. Torrential rain made the trek more arduous, as we trudged through mud for miles, ate gone-off fried meat in huts filled with ochre smoke, and pulled leeches off our clothes. There was no point whinging, and when I became homesick or worried about what lay ahead, I listened to music and re-membered why I was there. This was the first testing point of the Everest journey, and I'd stepped up to the mark.

Our first objective was a warm-up climb of the popular Mera Peak at 6,476 metres. First we reached Khare village, the same height as Mont Blanc, and I felt rotten enough that Francis delayed our summit bid for another rest day. That night, two dishevelled, Aussie climbers slogged up the wood-en staircase and collapsed into the dining room, having just summited that day.

"What was the worst part?" I asked quietly.

"All of it," they muttered. What was I getting myself in-to? Purna interrupted the silence with an impressive steamed cake complete with cherries on top.

"This Mera Peak summit cake!" Thoman grinned. His English was the best on the team but still not great. Perhaps we all felt the tension, but we could barely touch it. The cake came back to haunt us the morning after, when we smelled the rotten chicken from the week earlier. Purna had deep fried it for breakfast, and Kentucky Fried Cake is something I never want to experience again in my life. But it's the thought that counts. It was remarkable how they could create such things at that altitude whilst portering all the ingredi-ents and basic equipment. They were incredible, and their hospitality and willingness to go the extra mile for us was humbling.

Francis pointed out Everest on the way to Mera Peak high camp the next day.

"Excited yet?" he asked.

I didn't look. I was more concerned about the pain I was feeling whilst barely higher than Everest base camp. I hadn't drunk or eaten enough, or acclimatised well at all—a pretty undesirable combination. Pushing straight to high camp through deep snow involved almost one thousand metres of ascent, and the sudden height jump had concerned me.

I needed to weed the thoughts of failure from my mind as my body screamed for rest. This was meant to be the easy bit, and I was paranoid that Francis was watching me, about to call off my plans at the drop of a hat. Finally the slopes eased, and we saw one of the cook boys waiting for us with mango tea and biscuits. I made it to our camp well behind the others. Ongchhu and Phur Temba had pitched our tents, sparing us further pain, and I drifted into sleep satisfied that we'd got the worst part done.

I texted home with false confidence. "*Change of plan. Going summit 2moro. Call you on top of the bastard. Love Al.*"

I was awoken at 3:00 a.m. The summit push was on.

"Paul not coming?" Francis called out to Phil as we trudged through darkness towards the slopes. Paul stayed put. I was surprised.

I myself was incoherent and struggled to make it out of the tent without falling over, but I said nothing. A beautiful sunrise had never seemed so nauseating. After an hour or so, the winds picked up, but I lacked the foresight to put my thicker mitts on. I could barely move my toes, let alone in a coordinated fashion. I knew I could go no further. Francis was alarmed and said that this was dangerous. At just over six thousand metres, I was likely suffering from early onset high altitude cerebral edema, or HACE, a potentially fatal form of acute mountain sickness where the brain swells with fluid. We were heading down, and Phil soon retreated too.

Every few steps I stumbled over into the snow. I could hardly operate my jumar on the fixed rope. It was agonising, and I continued to tumble onto the snow. A similar situation on Everest could lead to death.

When we eventually reached the Mera La camp. I slumped against a sack of potatoes and drank in Diamox tablets for altitude sickness, rehydration sachets, and litres of water.

"If you don't recover by tomorrow, I'm calling a helicopter. No discussion," was all I heard.

That night at camp I managed a bleak text home. "*Worked so hard for this. Gave it everything but it's all over.*" Mum must have been having kittens.

I did recover. After degrading myself with every obscenity under the sun, I gathered some grit as we entered the Hinku Valley and camped by a frozen river. In the peace of my own thoughts, I decided Mera Peak didn't matter. I had no choice but to put it behind me; it was only the warm-up. I still didn't know how I would perform on a higher and harder peak, but I made sure I was hydrated, and somehow felt refocused and more determined than before.

Behind our tents were the remains of a teahouse that had been flattened by an avalanche just a week or so earlier, and the owner was apparently still buried inside. We tucked into the Nepali dish of lentils and rice, or Dahl Baht, beneath a tarpaulin shelter whilst Phur Temba teased a rat scuttling behind the cooker. None of it bothered me—there were bigger things at stake.

The next day, base camp was situated at 5,450 metres beside a glacial lake, dwarfed by a dazzling panorama of peaks and the majestic face of Baruntse herself. At 7,129 metres it was breathtaking, if not a little monstrous. This wasn't a dream but the real thing. Only three other expedition teams shared the spot with us, giving it a special mood. Whilst we stuffed our faces with biscuits in the tranquility of the dining tent, the Sherpas threw a near-empty canister of gas onto a fire, which produced an enormous bang that sent us running for cover behind our tents.

"Paul! Afghanistan!" Thoman shouted as flames shot into the air.

Thoman had earned himself the nickname "Blackadder," as he was frankly useless. He lacked the necessary authority, hence our mountain tents still hadn't arrived, and Francis was kept busy solving the various logistical problems. Our objective, climbing via the southeast ridge, was now uncertain. I was pissed off because the stakes were so high, but this was the nature of expeditions in challenging locations. I tried to remain positive. A recent cyclone had also rendered conditions far colder than they should have been. Word got to us that two Czech climbers were missing high on Baruntse. Temperatures below minus twenty-five degrees centigrade were now forecast on our summit day, and with the high winds, we only had two possible windows. Being British, we would follow the French team so they could do the hard work of breaking the trail through waist-deep snow.

We had fried-Spam-and-kerosene pasta for breakfast before we made the first foray to Camp One, at 6,100 metres, but now we couldn't stay there as planned. All day I whinged to turn back, probably because of our experience on Mera Peak, but the others encouraged me to dig deep. I would thank them later.

I was optimistic when we tried again for the actual summit a couple of days later. We only had one shot, and again, would be poorly acclimatised. All I could do was my best. Within fifteen minutes of leaving base camp, Paul had turned round, complaining of a bad knee and a chest infection. Below the steep technical cliff, about two hundred metres high, Phil sighed.

"Sorry guys, I'm done."

"What the hell am I still doing here?" I thought. But I listened carefully to my own body. Two days later we had settled at Camp Two, approximately 6,400 metres, in good order, and conditions were better than expected. Francis and I rested to brew ginger tea.

"The guys will be feeling pretty pissed off with themselves down there," he began.

I was disappointed my two teammates had abandoned their summit hopes, and questioned whether continuing without the whole team was correct. I couldn't believe it. I had never expected them to throw the towel in before I did.

"Is it normal to be out of breath?" asked Mum on the satellite phone that night. I told her not to ask stupid questions.

Summit of Baruntse from Camp Two

Through the opening in the tent door, I watched as a lone climber descended the final abseil and staggered into camp like I had just a week earlier. Baruntse was intimidating, but summit day was tantalisingly close. I felt the confidence, adrenalin, and excitement. Situations could change rapidly, but sometimes uncertainty is the best motivator. I drifted into a restless sleep.

"Jam jam!" called Ongchhu from outside—his version of "let's go!"

At 2:00 a.m., we set off from fixed ropes in the cold and began the assault up the ice wall. I'd left my energy behind in the tent. As I clung weakly to the slope, the pain was indescribable. Each pull on the jumar hurt but I couldn't pinpoint where. I wasn't ill this time, just exhausted. Only the head torch beam beckoned me upwards. I was facing failure, devoid of all motivation, drive, and mental resolve, but I didn't care anymore.

"I'm trashed," I cried out.

"No you're not. Come on!" Francis said from the darkness above.

I tossed all the motivational quotes and routines I'd relied on down the slope. Each crawl upwards felt like stubbing a toe on the edge of a door. I found myself kneeling to rest my head on the snow, whimpering out loud and looking down at the black abyss below. After two hours, at 6,600 metres, I knew it was time to turn around. Again.

Those final few hours back to base camp were excruciating. I was dangerously dehydrated, but I couldn't even pull off my Marmot down-insulated gear. I wanted to lie down on the glacier.

"Whatever you think, you've done well. You pushed further than anyone else," Francis told me.

I felt otherwise. I was wallowing in self-pity like a sunburnt recluse. I felt defeated, physically and mentally useless. I hadn't even contemplated this happening on the practice run. I wished I'd pushed on a little bit longer. Turning back was the right decision, though. If I had continued for the remaining hours on more technical ground, I dread to think

Camp near Baruntse

what state I'd have been in. We weren't even halfway to the summit.

In the coming days we crossed the Amphu Labsa pass and trekked down the valley to Lukla. Revived by the rich air in the paradise of the mountains, I tried to work out what card I would play next. I showered for the first time in twenty-six days back at the Thamel Eco Resort hotel in Kathmandu. We must have fumigated the dining room as we annihilated the remains of the free breakfast buffet. Our taste buds could barely handle the excitement.

As much as I'd wanted to reach the summit of Baruntse, not doing so was a blessing in disguise. Becoming a liability on a mountain is never an option. The experience was a rude awakening, and experience is what keeps us alive.

CHAPTER 15

I'll Stick Around

"No battle plan remains the same upon the first contact with the enemy."—Helmuth von Moltke the Elder

The bustling departure lounge of the Mumbai Airport was not the best place to think.

Now I would need every lashing of commitment and conviction to prove myself capable of a place on an Everest expedition. I hadn't had the best opportunity due to a catalogue of errors, but nobody was going to empathise with the harsh reality of mountaineering. To be accepted, I didn't have to summit, just prove myself capable above 6,400 metres, the same height as Camp Two on Everest. I assumed this criteria ruled me out straight away. Had I gone to climb Everest the next day, it was clear that I wouldn't be ready, psychologically or physically. I was told so at base camp, too. It hurt, but I couldn't deny the facts. Everest didn't give a damn how hard I had worked—grit and commitment alone didn't give me the right to stand atop a mountain. All I could manage were the factors in my hands, but the rest depended on a chain of events falling into the right place at the right time.

Looking at the expedition as a whole, rather than just the summit, would help me avoid disappointment. Baruntse had been a proper no-frills adventure far beyond the comfort zone where my self-doubts lurked. My definition of possible was ever-expanding. Every obstacle I'd overcome so far had given me strength and challenged my self-imposed limits. This one was no different.

In four months I'd be boarding the plane to Nepal for Everest. Could I really throw it all away? Abandon everything that I'd suffered for? My efforts would only go to waste if I didn't learn from them.

Above the city lights of London, the Jet Airways flight made its final descent into Heathrow. The cabin lights dimmed whilst the song "Miracle" blasted through my iPod. Right now, I needed it. Dad drove me home and I told him tales from the trip. I didn't want to hear I'd done well. It didn't qualify anything that had happened.

We were stopped at a motorway services when a relative called, concerned, to ask about my granddad. Panic took over. I rang home, hoping it was a misunderstanding. Mum finally answered with a faint voice and asked if I was close.

"Just bloody tell me! Is he okay?" I demanded.

She tried to pretend all was fine, but something was untoward. I heard her tears through the phone.

"He's passed away," she said.

It stung me silent. My face flushed pale with shock. I hung up. The next hours on the M6 motorway dragged like an eternity. When I got home, Mum opened the front door and threw her arms around me, sobbing.

Imagining life without Granddad left us reeling and torn. He'd collapsed from a heart attack whilst walking his dog in the park, dignified and doing something he took great pleasure in. Granddad was content and graceful in his eighty-one years, but that didn't make it much easier. He had been so excited to speak to me about the trip—he'd always given me his support and enthusiasm in heaps—and one day on the calendar meant he couldn't. The last laugh we shared would be the day I left. It broke my heart.

Never had life been such an emotional rollercoaster. Until I knelt by the door and Harley bounded into my arms, I felt nothing but grief. Harley's presence was the first miracle. But just as one life had been taken from us, another had been given. Mum had a little white bundle tucked in her arms. Hector was a cockerpoo puppy—a blend of a poodle and a cocker spaniel—and only weeks old. Right now, little Hector was the only thing that could brighten the grey skies and dreary autumn weather as he chewed his way through the wardrobe and stumbled down the stairs.

The post-expedition blues caught up with me and I had a decision to make. I went back to the other climbers who'd advised and inspired me thus far. They knew the mountains well. I trusted and respected them, and their honest opinions would hopefully give me some reassurance. Instead, they dealt another blow. Most advised me to delay my plans. I was obviously no good at altitude, they said. Everest was two thousand metres higher than I had been, and I didn't know how my body would cope with the extremes. After the first trial run, it didn't look promising either. I'd stared failure right in the eye, and it was just as ugly as I'd expected.

"To hell with the doubters," my friend Ste told me.

Yet all these people couldn't be wrong, and fear of giving up was not a good reason to continue. I had to make the right decision, and I really had no choice but to cut the ropes. The verdict was in.

I texted Chris. "*I think it's off.*"

My beliefs were thrown out of the window. Bereaved and disappointed, I could only see the negative. I knew I'd fail only when I admitted defeat, but I was already defeated.

The bullies, epilepsy, everything had won. I could hear them taunting me all over again. Waiting until 2015 to climb Mount Everest just didn't feel like a valid option, and few will understand why it was such a dilemma. Starting fundraising from scratch was overwhelming and unimaginable this far along, and if I lost momentum now I might never get it back. Everest had started as an innocent ambition and had taken over my life until there was nothing else. Making a new game plan when I'd already visualised the year ahead may not have been so bad, but I didn't want to find out.

For days the weight of the decision felt heavy. I remembered how at Baruntse I had outperformed stronger and more experienced climbers and learnt from my bad decisions. Surely this meant something? After all, we know our own capabilities better than anyone. Those who had doubted me hadn't been there. Other climbers gearing up for the 2014 Everest trip had surfaced in the circle and I was desperate not to be left behind. My friend Jeff Smith from Cardiff was marking his fiftieth year by attempting to reach the summit after climbing Manaslu, the eighth-highest peak in the world. His enthusiasm for life was infectious, and he was one of the few who still believed in me.

I did receive some encouragement. I received an email from a woman saying that her sixteen-year-old son was going to do a skydive for charity since I had proven to him that anything is possible if you put your mind to it. Others said nobody would think any differently of me whatever I chose next. Mum was broken, so I didn't trouble her. The decision was mine alone. Unfortunately, I'm awful at making decisions.

I carried on with business as normal and soon came to an answer. I believed I had more to give and could train harder to build on my many weaknesses. I couldn't bear to let Granddad down—the day before he died, he'd told Gran how proud of me he had been. Only then did it sink in that I'd never see him again, but I could almost hear him telling me, "Go on, lad!"

The path to Everest had brought me wonderful experiences, and I'd made a pact with myself to finish what I started, with no regrets. Trying and failing was surely better than not trying in the first place. Chris said he worried that falling short would destroy me, but if I believed I could, then I'd have to get on with it. Advice, after all, is just a reflection of one person's experiences in the world, and you only take it if it agrees with what you already wanted. Soon enough, the decision was made.

But first, I had to get on a team. I was certain I couldn't get a place on Tim's expedition, so I had already started to research other teams with the same caliber of logistics and leadership. Another expedition operator agreed they would happily have me along. Although they had a glowing reputation, they didn't offer the same level of support high on the mountain and imposed a lot of the decision-making on the members themselves. I had to decide before teams were fully allocated. There were only a few minutes to send the email and pay the deposit. I decided that if Tim wouldn't accept me with his understanding of the attributes needed, then finding another team could compromise my safety and values. Integrity came first, so I held back.

Anxious of waiting, I tried my best to continue building the campaign, knowing it could still fall apart. I half-heartedly returned to my routine and sent even more emails.

Tim finally returned from an expedition in December and was keen to chat. 2014 all came down to this one phone call. I made honesty my policy, and upstairs in my room, I explained what went wrong, and more importantly, what I'd learnt from it. Tim put me straight on the spot and asked if I believed I could do it. Was I resilient enough? Could I endure it? I answered confidently to each, and I trusted my answers. Whatever I was saying, it struck a chord, as he acknowledged I was on the right lines with my attitude by knowing what it takes and what I had to put into practice.

"Well, there's a place if you want it. The offer's there," he said.

I was elated and promised I wouldn't let him down.

"I'm on! I have a place!" I cheered downstairs, prancing around the room. Now it was my turn to throw my arms around Mum. She was relieved that I would be climbing with someone she knew.

I told my teammate Ellis that I hoped he didn't snore because I would be joining him at base camp. After all of this, whether I reached the summit or not, getting myself on the team felt like a success in itself. Appreciating how close I'd come to throwing in the towel reminded me to be patient. I'd need plenty for the sprint to the finish; technical skills and mental tenacity through mountain training became crucial, and if I didn't step up to the mark, my place in the expedition would be lost. Once again, I was confident I could up my game by condensing years of preparation into four months. There was zero margin for pissing about. I needed time, hard work, and one hundred percent discipline. Luck, or maybe a miracle, would take care of the rest.

CHAPTER 16

Miracle

"It always seems impossible until it's done."—Nelson Mandela

Four months gave me little time to condition my body for Everest, where it would have just one third of the oxygen at sea level. Another expedition was out of my reach financially. At sea level in Cheshire, there were no mountains nearby, or any way to train for such extreme altitude. Training for mountains was best done in the mountains, but getting to them every week wasn't always possible. I resolved to do everything that I could do to strengthen my body and train it to use oxygen efficiently. Whether it would make any difference high in the "death zone" remained to be seen. I couldn't live without exercise anyway, so it never became a chore. I walked with hefty rucksacks, cycled for hours through the night, and sprinted in the pool until I puked—and picked up Achilles tendonitis within a week of being home.

In the summer, Paul White had invited me to the ICE Adventure Challenge in Dorset, a collective of young people who would camp on Brownsea Island, cook dinner for adventurer Ben Fogle, and kayak across Poole Harbour. I was teamed up with Polar adventurer Oli Milroy, who became a good friend. Paul had also introduced me to his son, Ian, a professional hockey player and sports scientist at the University of Exeter. I emailed him straight away. He became my personal trainer and gave me a programme to follow until the day I left. Taking it too easy was as dangerous as overtraining, but I trusted his expertise would see me through. Once again, I decided to give up running. Another injury would be catastrophic to the expedition. Thanks to my physiotherapist, at least I had the choice. I returned to the hospital one day to drop off a thank-you card for him and was glad to leave it behind.

By the following Monday morning I was grinding away on my bike for forty miles. Cycling allowed me to push my body for longer without damaging it like running did. Training without breakfast depleted my glycogen stores and improved my ability to burn fat, but there was a lot of work to do. Only now did I appreciate what proper training felt like, outside of my comfort zone, building the necessary mental resistance. Forcing through the fierce winter with rain in my eyes and my toes going numb was brutal. Locals looked on as I cursed myself under the grey skies. Sometimes I took it too far.

"Please say you're not going out in this?" said Mum as a gale brewed outside.

Even better, I thought. If it was fun, I wasn't pushing hard enough. One freezing ride in the rain left me so exhausted and hypothermic that Mum collected me, shivering and slumped, from the roadside. Nobody would be able to pick me up on Everest.

I took great pleasure watching the postman attempt to deliver a twenty-five-kilogram kettlebell up our driveway. One of Ian's friends, Mitch, had given me a strength and conditioning programme. I despised strength training—I could barely produce two pull-ups. When lifting weights and lunging in the garden didn't hurt enough, I felt frustrated by my lack of technique, at least until my muscles got sore and I hobbled around like I'd been run over by a bus. I also hated swimming. I started doing my interval training on the bike. Ten reps of ninety-second maximum sprints uphill left me wheezing for breath. All the while I visualised the impending struggle up the Lhotse Face. Mollie, one of the other Everest climbers, had recommended isometric wall sits—sitting against a wall at a ninety-degree angle for as long as possible—which some sadistic individual had designed as a military disciplinary exercise. Monitoring my physical improvement eased the worries of the challenge somewhat.

Whilst some people popped bottles of champagne, my New Year started with a different kind of bang after I received a phone call from an organisation who had earlier promised me a five-thousand-pound grant towards the expedition. My lack of success on Baruntse meant that I had not met the conditions of the contract. How could an organisation that helped young people achieve their potential pull out now? But five thousand pounds was gone. Maybe the only thing I would climb was the Everest-sized mound of plates and pans at work. I was livid, but soon realised that as one door closed, another would swing open.

Now I had a huge deficit and weeks to make up for it. Fundraising soon took the novelty of training away. As the months slipped away, my training plan often left me writhing in the darkness of our living room, bracing myself for the uncomfortable hours ahead. I just had to do the best I could, though instead of lying there questioning myself, I often wondered whether Harley would survive until the morning. He'd suffered a stroke on a walk, and I started sleeping in the living room to keep an eye on him. As he grew more frail and his muzzle greyed, he developed a taste for sirloin steak and homemade pancakes, and getting him to eat was often the hardest thing we had to do each day. We knew this Christmas would be his last, and going away to Scotland meant I'd have to leave him behind.

Someone once said that Everest was good training for Scottish mountaineering. I hoped being out in the Scottish weather would break my soft spots and help me build my mountain skills, like getting used to operating gear with thick gloves on. The most innocent of mistakes, like a glove blowing away, can become a life or death situation when you start climbing at serious altitude.

I was uncomfortable venturing into the dangers of the Scottish mountains alone, and felt I would learn more in the company of experienced mountaineers. I had to find someone to suffer with me. After scouring the forums for climbing partners, I was soon climbing Ben Nevis at one in the morning with a guy named Lorn. I then climbed Beinn Ghlas, a more remote mountain near Loch Tay, with a guy called Pete, where we were swallowed by a full whiteout. Our faces burned from the wind, gusts swept up beneath our feet, and we ended up abandoning the summit just a hundred metres ahead; another important judgement call. I was beginning to understand why Scotland had earned such a fearsome reputation.

That night, as I stood outside alone in the pouring rain and howling wind, the warm glow of the Glen Nevis youth hostel seemed to beckon to me.

They say Everest is good training for the Scottish winter.

"Man up!" I ordered myself, walking straight past to pitch my tent in a field. There would be no youth hostel on Everest.

It reminded me of my A-level celebration walk. Chris and I had camped during a fierce gale on nearby mountain Cadair Idris, where legend said anyone who camped on the slopes would wake a madman, a poet, or dead. At least I was immune to the first two.

I had barely seen anything, though, until I went to the town of Aviemore to attend a winter mountaineering skills course in the Cairngorms National Park, home to the snowiest, coldest, and highest plateaus in the British Isles. Its reputation was almost as big as the mountains themselves. Venturing straight into blast freezers of the corries—huge bowls in the hillside—each day was brutal.

I spent plenty of time under canvas and living off the reduced-to-clear aisle in Morrisons supermarket, which was mostly packs of oatcakes and Soreen malt loaf. I was trying to make things as difficult as possible. I liked to think that I could manage whatever was thrown at me, although moving alone through the murky blackness of Glenmore Forest in the middle of the night had me running like a cheerleader in a horror film. I was glad to reach Ryvoan Bothy, an ancient stone mountain hut, for the night.

For my eighteenth birthday present, Mum and Chris had given me the choice of a car or the equivalent money towards my expedition—a clear no-brainer. I even opted for a mountain navigation course instead of a party. But as weather conditions changed so frequently, not having a car was now a major stump. The slightly tamer mountains of Snowdonia and the Lake District were easier for me to get to, and so I spent dozens of mournful mornings cycling to the train station, negotiating snowy plateaus with limited daylight, and navigating through mist as my map tore apart in the wind. I was surprised by how fierce the conditions could be just two hours away from home.

I still needed to get better at certain technical aspects, and I was glad to try several climbing routes in the Lake District with my Baruntse expedition leader, Francis. Crawling up snow gullies with snowdrift scratching at our eyeballs to wait on an exposed platform was miserable. After an arduous day of scrambling, and after we'd rescued his snowed-in car from the treacherous Kirkstone Pass, my friend Keiran said he'd bet his business that I had what it took. Likewise, James Ketchell, who'd climbed Everest in 2011, reassured me that to get as far as I had was a pretty good indication that, if conditions allowed, I had the determination and drive to reach the summit. Now I just needed to start believing that myself.

I was feeling more resilient all the time, yet back home, Harley continued to waste away and things were looking bleak. The vet explained that his kidneys had almost entirely failed. We had watched him struggle for long enough, and now we had to make the decision to end his suffering. We took him to the nearby duck pond, his special place, for the last time. As he lay down on the grassy bank, we knelt beside him and cried, savouring every second we had left. Mum didn't want to let the vet into our house that afternoon, but his time had come.

I will never forget the way Harley looked up in panic, the vet's sickening last words, "I'm injecting now," or how his pained gaze faded softly beneath my chin as I kissed him goodbye. Within seconds, his chest fell still, and he passed away peacefully.

"You're not climbing Everest," Mum sobbed. "I can't lose you too."

The house had never been so quiet. I dragged my heavy conscience on a thirty-four-mile training hike and reminisced on the countless happy memories Harley had left behind. He was a sensitive, gentle, and affectionate dog, who frequently destroyed my sock collection and was known to flee when dogs half his size yapped at him. The Everest mission felt lonelier than ever before. Harley and Hooch were

Alex and Harley

gone before they could see me at the finish line. I guess in a way I had one less thing to worry about now, but I still miss them every day.

Time was running out. I'd contacted nearly a thousand people by now, but the email I sent to a local networking rep, Paul Daniels, was my golden ticket. He introduced me to his database of contacts, which eventually brought me thousands of pounds in sponsorship. The prestigious Chester Business Club also booked me to speak at their next dinner to eighty plus people and appointed me as their Young Ambassador, even donating to my Everest charity fund. But it didn't stop there. I was introduced to John Thomson OBE, an executive coach, former brigadier in the British Army, and the deputy lieutenant for Cheshire. With a decorated military career and a passion for helping others achieve their potential, John stood out as a dignified man, and I was honoured to have his help with my motivational speaking and the specific challenges of my project. Over several sessions, John worked with me to fine-tune my presentation skills, and everything I learned turned out to be invaluable. He reassured me I had a compelling story already, and that was ninety percent of the battle.

When the business dinner came, I was paralysed with fear. Some of their previous speakers had been Lord Sebastian Coe and the Prime Minister, to name a few. I could not mess this up. My passion took over, and the audience hung on my every word as I told them about my journey. Strength rushed through me. My stammer barely bothered me for those thirty minutes, and when it did, I laughed and said, "Oh, that's my stammer just saying hello!" to the admiration of the audience. After the talk, they even gave me a standing ovation.

I raised a hand, just like I would when I reached the top of the world—I could have already been there. Adrenalin surged through my body as if I were free-falling. John smiled from the back of the room, and I smiled back, sharing the victory with him. Regardless of how much speaking scared me, hell, I wasn't going to run away from it anymore. I had absolutely no idea this one particular talk would prove to be one of the most important of my career.

From then on, the final weeks quickly came together.

"For trying... and not stopping... let's meet," said a local managing director, who, after emailing five times, agreed to sponsor the expedition with one thousand pounds. A local firm where one of my friends worked came on board with a further 2,500 pounds. There was still nearly ten thousand pounds to raise.

After months of pressing for a meeting, I went to the Macclesfield headquarters of a leading consumer finance technology firm, Quintessential Finance Group. Greg Cox, the CEO, was broad, tall, and full of enthusiasm as he entered the boardroom. Everest had always captured his imagination as a child, and as a young entrepreneur he had founded innovative businesses with up to sixty million pounds turnover. The stakes were high. By a stroke of luck, ITV News had arranged an interview hours earlier, so I stressed the urgency, and my passion took over to sell it.

"How old are you mate?" Greg asked.

"Eighteen," I said.

Smiling, he asked me to wait outside for a moment whilst they discussed the proposal. I could do nothing more. My heart froze. I had waited fifteen months, but the few seconds of pause felt like an eternity.

Greg smiled. "You've got a deal, mate."

I was in disbelief. Everest was on.

Pingtree and UK Loans, their major brands, had fitted the final brick in the wall. They were thrilled to be my second major sponsors and have their logos carried to the very peak of the world. Now I would finally get the chance. I was glowing as I shook their hands and tried to find the words to thank them. With just five weeks to go, the moment I'd waited for had come, although different from how I imagined. I can't tell you how good it felt.

I managed to skip past their office block twice on the way back to the train station, texting friends and sharing the news that they had eagerly awaited. As I ran down the street to Chris Spray's house at 10:30 p.m., I finally got to fulfil our gentlemen's agreement by dancing around the village with pants on my head.

Greg Cox, Alex, and Mike Ransom

"What the hell are you doing?" he asked, puzzled. I laughed and laughed, jumping around in circles.

"Hang on. Have you got it?"

"I'm going!" I cheered.

His face was a picture of pure delight. "Best get the coffee machine on then!"

Tackling the biggest hurdle allowed me to focus on my training, and even though fourteen-hour mountain hikes were no longer demanding, I spent the last weeks worrying whether I had trained enough. My expedition leader Tim would be watching me very closely. I started to feel there was no real purpose to the sessions, and as I cycled a hundred miles one morning, I lost my focus.

"Sod this," I whined. I turned round to head home.

I couldn't understand it, but on the phone, John Thomson calmly explained I was going through a "grey zone," as it was known in the army. I was no soldier, though. John agreed that I should stop training now, as when people try to correct a perceived physical deficit, they often get injured right before the event. I couldn't bear the thought; once I'd paid the full expedition balance, there were no refunds.

There was little more to do now. Life was good as it was. My final few weeks at home were spent catching up with family, testing my kit, liaising with sponsors, sending emails, and dealing with a barrage of media interviews and requests. I couldn't have been happier. In a top-of-the-range Land Rover, Greg's personal assistant collected me to give an impromptu talk to all of their staff and pose for a photo shoot.

Finally I could see and believe that Everest would be a reality. I couldn't lose respect for my goal, however—I still had lots to learn. Grandma was conscripted into sewing sponsor badges onto my kit until just hours before I left. My friends and family would face two sleepless months while I was gone, but they wanted this as much as I did. They'd been dragged through the same pitfalls and celebrated the peaks with me.

PART 4

FALSE HORIZON

CHAPTER 17

Living the Dream

"So, if you cannot understand that there is something in man which responds to the challenge of this mountain and goes out to meet it, that the struggle is the struggle of life itself upward and forever upward, then you won't see why we go. What we get from this adventure is just sheer joy. And joy is, after all, the end of life. We do not live to eat and make money. We eat and make money to be able to enjoy life. That is what life means and what life is for."—George Mallory

29th MARCH 2014

My whole life I never thought I'd achieved enough. Today was the exception. I gave one final glance at the Everest "Live the Dream" poster on my bedroom wall and felt the sensation of goosebumps on my arms. This was no longer a dream. This was the real deal. I was quickly realising that our dreams always take a different shape from what we imagine. There was none of the fanfare that I had anticipated, at least not yet. It was like any other day, except for the first time in fifteen months I had nothing to do except enjoy the experience ahead. I didn't know what to do with myself.

Gran and Mum looked pale and vacant as they stood in the terminal of Manchester Airport. If there was ever an opportunity for me to make some sort of noble, poignant statement, this was it. "See you in June!" wasn't very comforting. Mum always said that raising me was her biggest success, but right now, she probably wished I'd never tried paragliding those years earlier.

"Don't take any risks," she whimpered as she hugged me tight.

It was a promise I couldn't keep. Expeditions on any mountain were risky regardless of how many precautions were taken. "Risk nothing—gain nothing," I had learned from Bear Grylls when I met him just weeks earlier. He advised me not to have an ego, to respect the mountain, and to know when to turn around.

After one final sales pitch at check-in to waive my overweight baggage fee, I left my emotional baggage behind as the flight departed for Abu Dhabi. Kathmandu was unchanged since four months ago. The streets of Thamel district buzzed with life, and a sense of anticipation filled the air. I tried not to break an ankle in one of the potholes as we were bombarded with offers of rickshaw rides and bargain adventure trips. It was a miracle that more tourists weren't mown down by the taxis and scooters weaving throughout the city. Kathmandu boasted more outdoor shops than probably any other city in the world. Counterfeit North Face clothing lined the shop fronts alongside other tourist fodder, like Nepalese singing bowls, Khukuri knives, handcrafts, and Pashmina scarves. The Nepali people were charismatic and plainly dressed. Western and Asian tourists, mostly adventure seekers, browsed the sights as they prepared for their treks and expeditions.

After visiting the breakfast buffet four times, a familiar voice called out to me in the lobby of Hotel Manaslu.

"Young man!" said Tim, our expedition leader, coming over to shake my hand. Tim was in his late forties, but with four Everest summits under his belt, it didn't show in his neat, athletic appearance. At eighteen, I would be his youngest ever Everest team member, and the second youngest person on the mountain in 2014 besides a seventeen-year-old Australian. I had to read our expedition permit twice to prove my name was really there.

We grabbed lunch and sorted out last minute details. We received a briefing on new regulations at the Ministry of Tourism. Whilst their intentions were probably good, they were poorly conceived, and laughable at best. Expedition operators already had to pay a four thousand dollar deposit to remove their waste, and rightly so, but corruption often meant they didn't get it back.

The gulf between Western expedition operators and Sherpa operators had widened in recent years. The Sherpa were an ethnic group living in the Eastern regions of Nepal, mostly high in the Himalayas, and as such possessed great expertise. Some of the younger Sherpa thought there was no need for Western operators to organise expeditions on their mountain. They probably wanted to control the huge sums pouring in, but many of the locally led expeditions lacked the decision-making skills and logistical insight of the Western ones. Some of the Sherpa had earned their IFMGA mountaineering guide qualification and accordingly expected to be paid as much as the Western guides, but such income would only disrupt the balance within the ethnic Sherpa community.

Even with only two expeditions to Nepal stamped on my passport, it was clear to me that the local people were held in the highest regard by the climbers on Everest and other expeditions. Their involvement was paramount and we knew it, which is why they earned much more than the average income in the region. Towards the Sherpa the climbers felt great respect and gratitude.

Back in 2013, however, drama unfolded when three high-profile climbers clashed with Sherpas at Camp Two after what seemed like a simple misunderstanding. The kettle boiled over at last. The media sensationalised the situation, and the Daily Mail even referred to Swiss climber Ueli Steck as a "Mr. Woolly Stick." Under media scrutiny, the ministry announced a one thousand dollar increase in permit costs, which would provide a liaison officer for every expedition and a team of nine security personnel at base camp. It was jolly good in principle, but whether they turned up remained to be seen.

A Geordie voice interrupted my last minute blog writing in the hotel internet cafe.

"Alex, buddy, we meet at last!"

I spun round to see my teammate Ellis J. Stewart smiling. It felt like we'd known each other for a long time even though we had only spoken online.

In his mid-forties, Ellis was married with three kids, and ran a small adventure sports merchandising company in his hometown of Hartlepool. He didn't have cash to burn either. He had pursued this longer than I had been alive with the most determination I have ever seen. With his calm demeanour, untidy dark hair, and broad shoulders, Ellis fit the mountaineer stereotype far better than I did. Regardless of our differences, we shared the same dream, and now we were going to live it together.

Crammed inside the Sita Air turbo-prop plane, I couldn't resist smirking as the flight attendant pointed out the emergency exits. Fortunately, the pilot had his Weetabix that morning, and as we touched down in Lukla, the adventure had begun. After a breakfast of apple pancakes and boiled eggs at the Paradise Lodge teahouse, Tim came in with a serious expression.

"Alex, there's been some confusion. One of the porters from a Mera Peak expedition has taken your bag by mistake!" I was horrified, until he burst into laughter.

The three of us set off along the trails as the others would join us later. Porters carried our kitbags closely behind, and our guide Laxman, who looked much younger than his mid-twenties in his stylish green sunglasses, led the way. Following in the historic footsteps of Sir Edmund Hillary and Tenzing Norgay on their ascent over sixty years ago felt surreal, albeit less so when we passed an imitation Starbucks coffee shop and YakDonald's cafe. We baked in the humid sunshine amongst the dazzling hues of rhododendrons and magnolia flowers. Huge suspension bridges crossed lush farmland, overhanging cliffs, and quaint villages. The fierce Dudh Kosi River cut into the valley below as we ascended. The cattle-like Dzo ("Zok-ee-oh") carried loads up to base camp as the herder hollered behind them. Porters heaved everything from gas canisters to crates of Coca-Cola on their backs, laughing with each other as they raced past. Colourful Mani stones inscribed with prayers were littered at the roadside below long lines of prayer flags, pieces of rectangular cloth that blessed the countryside and promoted good fortune.

The village of Monjo, at 2,835 metres, was our first stop. For the first two weeks we enjoyed the comfort of teahouses. These cosy, rustic establishments were all run by Sherpa families. They made their money from the over forty thousand trekkers and tourists entering the Khumbu Valley each year. Those trained with mountaineering skills worked on expeditions as climbing Sherpas, safeguarding and assisting other climbers on the mountain or carrying loads and setting up camps. The Sherpa were renowned for their hardiness and expertise at high altitudes. They possessed unique adaptations that allowed them to live and work at high altitudes, such as an improved haemoglobin-binding capacity and doubled nitric oxide production. Those traits, plus their strong minds and work ethic, gave them incredible power on the mountains that few Westerners, if any, could match. Many others worked as expedition cooks, assistants, trekking guides, and yak herders. The porter jobs usually went to younger men hoping to progress the ranks.

Most teahouses were furnished with wood. Glass cabinets were filled with out-of-date Snickers bars, bottles of fizzy drink, and various other luxury items. With the warm hospitality, it was hard to feel homesick. Teahouse cuisine was basic, a little monotonous at times, but considering our location, all of the food was impressive. Amongst the staples of rice, noodles, potatoes, and their interpretations of Western and Japanese cuisines (including comical spelling errors) were local delicacies like momo dumplings, Tibetan bread, and the local dish Dahl Baht, which tasted like burnt soup no matter how often I tried it. They even had deep-fried Mars bars. Eggs and occasionally tinned tuna were the main sources of protein besides yak meat. We definitely didn't go hungry—I even put on a few extra pounds.

As we moved higher up, the toilets would become a simple long drop—you didn't want to spend too much time there. It taught me to zip my mobile phone securely in my pockets. Trekking life was sleepy and relaxed. At night Tim would beat us at card games before we retired to our bedrooms, usually by 8:00 p.m.

Breakfast was always early. We dined on fresh chapatti bread and several cups of sweet milk tea, and twice a day I took a shot of concentrated beetroot juice. It was vile, but the high nitrate content supposedly increased oxygen in the blood and improved acclimatisation, so I held my nose and down it went. I had learned the importance of hydration from Baruntse. At a high altitude, the body requires much more water as it tries to get rid of excess alkali. Failure to drink enough early on would get us to base camp in bad order.

On day two we got our first glimpse of Everest through the trees. Her saw-toothed crest was engulfed in the fierce winds of a jet stream, for which we would wait weeks at base camp to clear. Almost all expeditions in the region passed through Namche Bazaar, making it the most expensive place in Nepal. It was an affluent village with houses and lodges of all sizes spilling up the hillside. It was the closest thing to home we would see for a while. We even caught up with the hype back home on the Wi-Fi connection.

Reading the influx of support and encouragement from people on social media gave me a huge boost and lifted my mood every day. I have always been touched how these people, some of whom I'd never met, had grown into a devout following of friends who rooted for me all the way. Chris had been raising my profile on Twitter as a way to encourage charity donations and build awareness. I felt as if it was my duty to succeed, like I'd been lifted onto some sort of pedestal, but it was never about fame; it was about sharing the suspense, struggles, and successes to hopefully inspire people. I would only get to share it once, after all.

Tim arrived at the teahouse for lunch shortly after. "How are you guys feeling?" he asked. We nodded.

"Ellis, you were going too fast. And Alex, you were going too fast," he said. We sat like naughty schoolchildren. He had been testing us for our benefit. The first one to base camp was usually the first to get a headache, he said. There was no rush, and taking nearly three weeks to acclimatise allowed us to appreciate this truly magical part of the world.

The Himalayan Experience team sitting nearby moved with more haste. Led by New Zealand mountain guide Russell Brice, HimEx were the best known and most influential expedition at base camp every season. Their group of clients were the A-Team on the hill; they looked elite and super-fit, and I felt like the class nerd. The disparity was quite clear. You could almost feel in the air how a good handful of the climbers were eyeing each other up as competition rather than bonding. I was proud to be on my team even if my youth gave them something to poke fun at. I had to remember that only I could put one foot in front of the other.

CHAPTER 18

Shot Down in Flames

"I am an old man and have known a great many troubles, but most of them have never happened."—Mark Twain

The village of Kyangjuma was home to little more than Ama Dablam View Lodge, ran by Tashi and Lakpa Sherpa, a former climber who had built the establishment by hand. A little spectacled lady in a long purple apron and black down jacket burst outside. The welcome was fit for a king.

"Tim!" squealed Tashi, her arms outstretched.

From their crowded kitchen, staff brought trays of biscuits, prawn crackers, and donuts, which we washed down with enough fresh filter coffee and tea to give us heart palpitations.

I woke to see the peak of Ama Dablam dominating the skyline. Tashi and Lakpa's lodge was so successful that they were able to visit the United States every year during the monsoon season in Kyangjuma. Tashi mothered us, giving us heaping portions of food and tying silk khata scarves around our necks for good luck. She had a heart of gold. I reflected on the incredible kindness of the Sherpa as we trekked through Khumjung village in the morning sun, sweat dripping down my back.

We stopped for afternoon tea, enjoying hot lemon and coconut biscuits opposite the tiny airstrip of Syangboche Airport, which was really just a trimmed field with stray dogs and expedition cargo piled up at one side. As we moved along the woodland trails we took in the Buddhist paintings and the silhouettes of jagged peaks. Mountain goats wandered the hillsides, but there were very few trekkers in sight. We stopped for lunch at Thamo, and our river crossing took us to Thame, a sleepy, charming village at 3,750 metres where the next member of our team, Chris, waited to meet us at Valley View Lodge.

Chris Handy was from Sheffield, like my dad. His wit shone through along with his extensive mountaineering experience. I enjoyed the Wi-Fi at the lodge and was finally able to post updates online. Dad had tried texting me various ways before I lost my patience and donated the wretched device to one of the porters. I was frustrated by my failure to plan. Mum pleaded for me to stop worrying, but she didn't understand the necessity for me to post updates to fulfil the marketing return for my sponsors. It couldn't become a distraction—I was trying to climb Mount Everest, after all—but my sponsors were the means to achieving my dream, and I was obligated to post updates for them. Unlike some climbers who wracked up debts from shaky sponsorship deals, I'd already received the sponsorship money. I couldn't just run away with it and forget my responsibilities.

I would have had an easier time as a monk living in the Thame monastery, one of the oldest in the Khumbu Valley, tucked beneath the surrounding nest of peaks. The monks, who took vows of celibacy and isolation, intrigued me. A monk dressed head-to-toe in a red gown ushered us inside a dimly-lit building decorated with faded religious paintings. An intricate, hand-carved altar covered one wall, and the smell of burning juniper filled the room. The Puja blessing was a traditional Buddhist ceremony for safe passage in the mountains. We sat cross-legged on the ancient wooden floorboards whilst the monk recited the chants, barely stopping to breathe. This remarkable ritual dragged on until he threw rice at us after whacking a large drum long enough that I needed to bless my hearing, too.

Most nights there was nothing for us to do. Tim mentored us in everything from high altitude medications to frostbite prevention and death on the mountain. He had seen loss of life high on Everest, and a lot of this was the result of neglect, misconduct, and incompetence. The prospect of encountering death for the first time didn't rattle me too much, as being with such a well-equipped team minimised the risk compared to the reward. I didn't know if I'd feel the same when I passed the dead bodies on the mountain, frozen solid in their lonely graves after risking it all to "live the dream" themselves. If we encountered seriously ill climbers on the mountain, it was up to our own discretion to get involved. Individual survival at such extreme altitudes is difficult enough, and especially above Camp Four. When descending, you are more susceptible to the debilitating hypoxia of altitude, cold, and increasing exhaustion. For the same reason, many bodies remain where they fell. Rescuing the ill or retrieving bodies is difficult and dangerous, almost impossible for one person alone. Whether they made the right decisions or neglected their safety was irrelevant. They might have been sons, parents, or husbands to someone, but so was everyone else.

Other trekkers in the dining rooms often overheard the discussions and asked questions in awe. Tim was always hesitant to elaborate, and I couldn't understand why. We had fought hell and high water to be here; we had every right to share it with anyone interested. He always said that we were "trying to climb Everest," rather than "climbing Everest," which I perceived as negative, but we would soon understand for reasons we had never anticipated.

At Maralung, a three-hour trek along the river, we saw little evidence of humans, let alone trekkers to ask questions. A beautiful Sherpani named Ang Chutin ran the lodge with her elderly mother. She tended to the herd outside, looked after her family, and cooked for trekkers, using just a one log fire and a tardis of a kitchen to produce amazing food. Even nearly halfway up Everest, the Sherpa stew, or Shyakpa, was delicious, loaded with fresh vegetables, potatoes, and dumplings. Ang Chutin would walk for a full day and back to the local market to buy the ingredients. She had developed impeccable English from the trekkers who stayed with her. Away from the basic amenities of running water and solar-powered electricity, the lodge was rustic, with fading mountaineering photos decorating the walls, tacky floral posters, and a cast-iron stove to burn yak dung for the plunging evening temperatures. There was little else besides the cattle herd grazing outside, who popped their heads through the door to watch the guys annihilate me at card games.

Being in the wilderness made me a little homesick, too. Self-doubt and negative thoughts crept in first. Was I strong enough? Did I have what it takes? If I couldn't relax, the mountain would tear me apart. I carried the negative thoughts on a hike up a nearby hill to kick-start the acclimatisation process the next morning. At five thousand metres, my headache was soothed somewhat by the sight of Cho Oyu

Maralung

which was the sixth highest mountain in the world. Towering ramparts of frozen stone, combined with scars of grey moraine on the sweeping valley below, could stimulate even the most fatigued minds on long days of trekking.

One thing my training hadn't corrected was my inefficient dallying with gear, which I learned the next day as we raced to pack our bags and get to breakfast before Tim could chastise us for being late. "Concurrent activity" were his buzzwords. Delays down here were insignificant, but they'd be detrimental higher up where the altitude makes everything take longer.

Moving at my own pace was key, and I knew Tim was testing whether I was foolish enough to keep up with him. Hours later, Ellis groaned his way onto the crest of the Renjo La Pass ahead of me.

"Bloody hell!" he said.

"Bloody hell!" I followed.

Learning was a delicate balance at altitude. Now I was drinking plenty, but too quickly. My legs had remained robust so far, and I didn't think about whether I had trained enough since Baruntse. We'd likely lose a huge amount of our muscle mass by summit day anyway—not that I had much to begin with.

We reached the serene village of Gokyo, home to the highest freshwater lake system in the world at 4,750 metres. At the Namaste Lodge, Japanese trekkers slurped noodle soup in the corner, cocooned in woolly hats, gaiters, gloves, balaclavas, and down jackets. The four porters arrived fresh-faced after hauling our kitbags and sat nearby. Tim bought them biscuits, which they always offered to us. Their physical prowess put me to shame.

I got chatting with two American climbers who were attempting both Everest and Lhotse, the fourth-highest mountain in the world. Making friends to share the journey with was special, especially when they took me seriously. My age was always the first question, as I was a gangly teenager covered in corporate logos like a walking billboard.

We saw the peaks of Cholatse and Thamserku on the horizon as we passed the crumbling structures of stupa shrines. We then arrived at Phortse village in time for afternoon tea. As we relaxed after dinner, someone replaced the CD of Buddhist chants on the stereo with a Nirvana album the very moment a local monk walked in and sat down. The irony was unbelievable.

In a few hours we made it to Pangboche, a historic village home to many of the Sherpas who worked on Everest. They could walk from there to base camp in just one day with ease, and I bet they never had to do wall squats, hill sprints, or cycling. I felt strong as we pressed on to Dingboche, and a day later, trudged uphill to the most impressive campsite I had ever seen. It stood over the Imja Khola valley, parallel with the north face of Ama Dablam and in front of the cliffs of Baruntse. The silence was sublime. I got sick our first night there. Perfect timing. Our Camp Two cook, an older Sherpa called Pasang Temba, brought me a tray of fluorescent mango juice, which I forced down gratefully as the staff busied themselves setting up camp.

Dorje Gyalgen sat on a boulder nearby with immaculate Julbo sunglasses and hair styled into a modern 'do. The year earlier he had partnered with legendary mountaineer Kenton Cool on an epic, record-breaking trio: climbing Everest, Nuptse, and Lhotse in one effort. After a sleepless night trying to pee into a bottle in the dark, I lay in my tent for most of the following day. Pasang Temba looked concerned when I turned away his plate of Dahl Baht, renowned as one of the best in the valley. He could have been crying, but the acrid kerosene fumes in the cook tent had my eyes watering too.

Losing my cool because of altitude sickness was all too easy. *Not again,* I cursed. Our itinerary allowed us to acclimatise slowly, so only my body was to blame. It was hard not to feel cheated, like my training would have been better spent playing chess.

Tim shot me down.

"If you have doubts, the mountain will exploit them, and if you doubt yourself you'll be going home in a week—and that's not because I'll send you home," he said.

I nodded weakly, furious at myself. How I felt now was irrelevant to how I'd feel on the mountain in a few weeks. Crossing the Kongma La Pass at 5,545 metres would acclimatise us above the height of base camp, and it was better to be ill here than in a few days' time. Determined to redeem myself, I dragged my lethargic body up and over the pass the next day. The relentless slope took us down towards the bleak rivets of moraine below, and each one of my steps hurt. Tim congratulated me at the bottom.

Lobuche was a blot on the landscape at 4,940 metres. The shabby collection of lodges was as gloomy as the Kala Patthar Lodge where we stopped to eat. Not long after, Laxman came over to the table, his usual smile gone. The calm mood in the teahouse tensed.

"I have bad news. Big avalanche on Everest Icefall," he said in broken English. "Six Sherpa die."

Tim cursed.

"Nine Sherpa missing," Laxman added.

That explained the helicopters flying over the valley towards base camp all day. The shock in Tim's face was clear as he pried for more information. Some of our own team's Sherpas were due up on the mountain that day. Tim wanted to rush to base camp straight away, but knew I was too ill to be left alone and hurried off to ring Iswari, our agent in Kathmandu. Ellis looked spooked. He said this was enough to make him abort.

I lay in bed and tried to understand what this would mean. Hours later, Ellis knocked on the door with horror in his voice. Thirteen Sherpas had been killed. Three were still missing, the highest death toll in Everest history. We knew little else, but knew it wasn't looking good.

CHAPTER 19

Icefall

"Many people pray to be kept out of unexpected problems. Some people pray to be able to confront and overcome them."—Toba Beta

19ᵗʰ APRIL 2014

My dreams were sweet, but I woke up in reality. I was strangely calm. The disaster was hard to comprehend, so I treated the day like any other, following the trail through boulders as helicopters whizzed overhead. Excited trekkers, some keeled over from the altitude, were as oblivious to the disaster as the herds of Yaks on the path. We were excited and uncertain at the same time.

Tim had promised to do everything he could, like acclimatising on the nearby mountain Pumori instead, to reduce the risk of time spent exposed in the Khumbu Icefall, which we had to pass in order to reach the first of the four camps before the summit. We knew it was dangerous. The avalanche had been caused by a serac, an enormous overhanging block of glacial ice, that had suddenly fallen from the west shoulder of Everest into the Icefall from about 5,800 metres. One of the ladders on the steeper sections of the route had broken, trapping a large number of Sherpa below the worst possible area. Huge chunks of ice thundered down and crushed them. Eight survivors were pulled out, some with serious injuries, and evacuated by helicopter to Lukla or Kathmandu. High altitude porters and climbers had left early that morning to ferry equipment and continue setting up camps. Teams of Western climbers were only a couple hundred metres behind, and IMG, International Mountain Guides, had a large number of climbers already at Camp One above. We were just days from following suit. Our staff had escaped injury, but from listening to the guides, we gathered that they knew one of the victims, Dorjee Khatri, very well.

Nestled on the Khumbu glacier, the tent city of Everest base camp was hard to see once snowfall clouded the valley. Tiny specks eventually appeared on the horizon. I had never really imagined how base camp might look, but I didn't expect it would take so long to get there. Moving at 5,350 metres was exhausting enough—my headache and dry throat were the least of my concerns. It was impossible not to trip on the rock and ice sheets underfoot. Trying to find our own camp amongst the maze of tents took a while. The site contained 350 climbers in the various teams and nearly six hundred staff, including Sherpa and other Nepali people. The atmosphere was solemn. Very few people stood around in the heavy snowfall, but one porter chirped, "Namaste!" as he passed. This simple gesture meant the world right then.

The Himalayan Guides camp had none of the fancy branding. Three rectangular tents and two small dome tents were contained in the little dip, perhaps a quarter of a football pitch. Our sirdar, Kame Nuru Sherpa, a respected elder from Pangboche, showed us to our tents hidden over a rocky lip. I unpacked into my new home, a yellow North Face two-man tent. We were thawing out in the cook tent when a soft-spoken, suave-looking man came inside and smiled.

"Good to have you guys here. We've got the full team now," he said, the disaster still etched clearly on his face.

The day earlier, Dr. Rob Casserley had rushed into the Icefall in a desperate attempt to help the victims. His wife Marie-Kristelle, a Canadian cardiologist, had rushed to the

Himalayan Rescue Association tent to prepare the medical kits and assist the injured Sherpas who were coming down from the Icefall. After dealing with the most serious cases, she had spent the rest of the day at the upper helipad of base camp certifying the deaths, as the victims were lowered by long-line. With the extent of traumas suffered, the calls were easy. Having both Rob and MK's expertise gave us peace of mind. Rob had also summited Everest a remarkable eight times, and I took an instant liking to him.

The day earlier, most of our team had woken to a frightening rumble at about 6:45 a.m., then watched in horror as the victims' bodies were airlifted down, one by one. Most of the Sherpas had already returned to their villages to grieve. They all knew each other, and their tight-knit community would be badly affected. A four day period of mourning had been announced, and the tragedy had certainly sobered the mood.

Our mess tent served as our team's living room. Tim was just one of three expedition leaders under the Himalayan Guides umbrella, and our team of five shared the same facilities with the other leaders and their own team members, making us fifteen strong. Scott Mackenzie was the fourth climber with Tim. He was easy-going and likeable, and had summited Broad Peak, one of the world's fourteen eight-thousand-metre peaks. Scott and Chris would try to climb without supplemental oxygen, a feat well beyond my imagination. Unfortunately for him, our team permit misspelled his name as "Scoot," which stuck for the rest of the trip. Like Scoot, Andy James was from London, a cheerful man with a handshake that nearly broke my fingers. Also from London were Daniel Wallace, an enthusiastic and highly-motivated surveyor, Nigel Briant, who quietly observed in the corner, and Lucy Rivers Bulkeley, or Bulks, as she preferred to be called. Bulks was great fun to be around and hard as nails, having been the first European woman to run the Four Desert Grand Slam and climb four of the seven highest summits on each continent. I sat awkwardly in the doorway and felt like I stuck out.

My toes were frozen in my sleeping bag the next morning. The spectacular sunrise took my breath away before I had to traipse across the field to breakfast in the mess tent. Waking each day below the peaks of Pumori, Lingtren, and Khumbutse never failed to amaze me; it was hard to believe the beautiful mountains could have caused a tragedy, but the Icefall looked deadly towering over base camp. The camp's valley was situated on a moving glacier, hemmed in by the walls and nooks of Nuptse and the west shoulder of Everest on either side. I looked up uneasily and couldn't comprehend why anyone had made the route through it. I guess there was little alternative.

After breakfast we met Henry Todd, our base camp manager, a man with broad shoulders, a distinguished face, and thinning hair. He was an expedition veteran and strong as an ox. Years earlier he had reportedly spent a week on Everest's South Col, the final camp before the summit, with just a couple packs of biscuits. Like Kame, he had also been on the support team for Bear Grylls when Bear reached the summit in 1998. The tent fell silent as Henry, or the "Toddfather" as he was sometimes known, helped himself to a sweet from the table.

We were told the controversy would blow over in a few days, to keep our heads down, and to be very careful with the blogging, as one climber was now a wanted man. Later it emerged that Joby Ogwyn, the American mountaineer who was due to wing-suit jump off the summit, had tweeted about carrying on climbing. This slip-up had badly upset some Sherpa, and Joby made a hasty escape out of base camp. I rang home straight away and stressed the importance of going incommunicado for a few days. Ste and Chris were already manning my Facebook and Twitter accounts very cautiously.

We soon heard that Alpine Ascents International, AAI, had already cancelled their expedition. Having lost five Sherpa in the avalanche, they felt they could not continue. It was a worry, as they were one of the biggest expeditions, but we were otherwise in good spirits. Base camp life carried on as normal as possible.

"Hey, Bulks! Alex is giving you a show!" Roman jeered as I stood in a basin of hot water and scrubbed the dead skin from my legs. Our Brazilian teammate Roman Romancini always lifted the mood with his boyish energy. He worked for a huge software company and was outgoing and full of enthusiasm. This was his third attempt on Everest. His last had fallen apart just weeks before departure after a serious bike accident left him with severe injuries. He'd had to learn to walk again.

The temperature plunged to negative ten degrees centigrade as we played charades in the mess tent after dinner. Base camp was quiet as tranquil tents lit up across the glacier beneath the dazzling stars. Our new home was beautiful, but in the darkness, some of our new neighbours had begun to forge very different plans.

CHAPTER 20

Retribution

"Sometimes it takes a natural disaster to reveal a social disaster."—Jim Wallis

21st APRIL 2014

The situation at base camp was tense, and the biggest uncertainty was whether the Sherpas would return, and if they did, would they be willing to work. Three of the victims remained lost on the mountain, and walking over their brothers would be bad karma to the deeply religious Sherpa. We had to respect their decision either way.

Ellis and I headed out for an acclimatisation hike. Standing on Kala Patthar gave a classic postcard view of Everest, but this time it didn't feel right. My awe turned to fear. I could barely look. Would it let us climb this year? Something about it was unsettling.

Down at Gorak Shep, we found a faint internet connection and browsed the website of philanthropist and mountaineer Alan Arnette, our most reliable hub of knowledge. People thousands of miles away seemed to know more than us. Back home, the media was declaring the season off. Teams remained on hold as the mourning period had now extended to seven days, but one article was very disconcerting. The Sherpa had produced a list of thirteen demands to the Ministry of Tourism. These ranged from increased insurance coverage to a ten-fold increase in payouts for the deceased, and rightly so—but the staff demanded to receive their pay even if they decided not to climb this season. It was a catch-22. The deadline for agreeing to these demands was April 28th, or they would stop climbing. The mourning period would end on the same date. A political agenda was hijacking the tragedy.

We barely exchanged a word as we trekked back to camp with our heads down, paranoid that tents had already started disappearing. There was a bald man in orange trousers and a fluffy Cintamani parka eating biscuits in the mess tent, who introduced himself as Ingo. Ingolfur Axelsson was famous back in Iceland. Relaxed and confident, he became a good friend and confidant. Ingo was climbing under Henry Todd's supervision with Paul Valin, a brawny, bearded French rugby player who was great fun, too.

Chris came in later on to say he'd been to see Henry and there was good news. All Henry had said was, "Just be glad there's good news."

We continued waiting, passing the time with banter, hanging around, and sheltering from the heat of the sun. Rob arrived looking defeated. He said he felt more optimistic walking round with Henry than he did when he came back to camp, but we could only assume why.

We heard Jagged Globe, a large British team, was on the brink of heading home. Teams were dropping like flies and we were losing control. All we could do was wait and see. There was little point worrying about something I had no control over. Lying in my tent, I remembered how things had miraculously turned in my favour on Baruntse.

22nd APRIL 2014

Many people attended the Puja ceremony to mourn the dead, but at the end, the sombre mood was hijacked into a political rally. The antagonists were mostly a small group of young, vocal renegade Sherpa, who exploited the emotion of the crowd to get their voices heard. Things were becoming increasingly militant. There was little unity, but they claimed to have a petition of three hundred names, in which peer pressure had undoubtedly played a role.

Things took a bizarre twist when one of the agitators was identified as the head Sherpa for one of the leading Western expeditions, and two of the demands on the list had been created by the leader of one of the locally led Nepali expeditions. This revealed that some IFMGA-qualified Sherpa guides and Nepali expeditions wanted Western guides out, and why some gave us little regard. It was unsurprising that the community felt betrayed by their government, but since the Western expedition leaders had looked after them and rallied on their behalf to increase their insurance, it was a bit of a stab in the back. There were better, if harder, ways to resolve the situation, but unfortunately for us, it lay in the government's hands.

The team was still waiting for good news of a resolve, so our Puja blessing was a half-hearted occasion.

Base camp was divided. Rob came back from the meeting none the wiser, joined by our final team member, Tim Calder, a quiet man from the Lake District with whom I got on well. An ex-Gurkha, Tim had spent twelve years in Nepal and said he would be very surprised if this didn't sort itself out, considering many Sherpa still wanted to work. He said we were in the best possible hands with Henry and Kame, so I put my trust in them. Every day we barely saw them as they worked their backsides off to try and come to a resolution with other teams. Once the perpetrators were ironed out, leaders had demanded "guns and handcuffs" to arrest them and resume the season, but the critical mass to achieve this was fast slipping away. The waiting game continued.

As I searched for a phone signal outside later that night, I was interrupted by beams from several head torches.

"Alex!" called a voice. It was Dorje Gyalgen.

"How are you, my friend?" he asked, shaking my hand warmly. I asked after his family.

Close behind were Jhyabu and Padawa, an eighteen-time Everest climber. I punched the air in the mess tent. The Sherpas return was surely a good sign, but I was told they had to come back for the Puja anyway.

23rd APRIL 2014

The next morning we had a Puja blessing, a Buddhist ceremony for safe passage in the mountains, which the Sherpa will not climb without. It was still a good sign, by any standard, that the climbing might continue. To their credit, expedition leaders Russell Brice and Phil Crampton flew to Kathmandu for an emergency meeting with the Ministry and returned optimistic, but IMG had already announced their departure, claiming their Sherpas did not want to work. Another Canadian team cited the instability of the Icefall as the reason for pulling out, but most of the leaders had agreed that the mountain was no more dangerous than usual.

Henry came in to update us that night looking thwarted. Intimidation was taking over, he said. Just a few ringleaders had managed to turn the rest into a mob and shut the entire mountain down in retribution. The Sherpa at base camp had been told that if they accompanied us or continued working, their legs would be broken, or worse. In Nepal, these threats are taken very seriously. Expedition operators would not risk torched villages or harm to defenceless people they had worked with for many years. Essentially they were holding everyone to ransom by threatening their own people. For the first time, I watched as the hopeful mood in the mess tent changed to one of anger. The bottled tension was released as two of the team verbally laid into each other. We frantically sent blogs and articles to get the truth back home, hoping it would turn things in our favour. The public had been kept in the dark and told that a straightforward Sherpa strike was underway. This strike had a malicious twist.

Some teammates proposed that between us, HimEx, and a few allied teams, we had the manpower and resources to fix the remaining route, even though the rope supplies had been moved to Gorak Shep. But this was a huge undertaking. All eyes were on Russell Brice. If he pulled the plug, everyone would follow. In 2012, the threat of the very same deadly serac had unnerved him enough to cancel his expedition. The Adventure Consultants team announced they were going too, and our strength in numbers declined further. Even reverting to an old-school approach—spreading the burden of load-carrying amongst the members—would allow us to proceed with the few collective Sherpas who might be willing to work. Our Sherpa staff had returned willing to climb, at least until their loyalty was also overridden by the threats. Even if we climbed on our own, they would still be vulnerable. The idea of taking a stand the next day in hope that others would follow was quickly dismissed.

Bhim's yak cheese pizza went untouched. I felt sick. I lay confused in the solitude of my tent. Unlike the other obstacles on this ill-fated journey, there was no solution. The feeling of powerlessness was unprecedented. It was like being bullied all over again. I couldn't even face writing my daily diaries—but what happened next would remain etched in my memory.

CHAPTER 21

Biting Hands

"An eye for an eye will only make the whole world blind."—*Mahatma Gandhi*

24th APRIL 2014

In a last-ditch attempt to reclaim the mountain, the government sent a representative to negotiate. The Nepalese Minister of Tourism, Bhim Acharya, arrived by helicopter with a delegation of officials. After trays of food were taken in to the SPCC tent for breakfast, they eventually came out to face the crowd of over two hundred Sherpa, sirdars, leaders, and climbers. I watched from a safe distance. It reminded me of a *Monty Python* scene, and I half expected the crowd would stone him if he said "Jehovah."

According to eyewitnesses, the atmosphere at the meeting was not pleasant as they addressed the crowd. The minister waved his magic wand and declared the mountain open. He was, of course, blissfully unaware of the threats taking place, and the Sherpa probably didn't trust him anyway. He had also reportedly agreed to the demands, which would have been a good thing if one of the demands wasn't to get their pay cheque even if they closed the season.

The proceedings finished and I watched the crowd disperse. Moments before the delegation could board their helicopter, another block of ice broke loose from the west shoulder of Everest. Another avalanche thundered into the Icefall, the same place where the first had taken sixteen lives. I looked up in disbelief as my hopes were buried beneath it. Regardless of superstition that Chomolungma was indeed a goddess, the timing could not be coincidental. Cheers followed the crashes as I retreated behind the mess tent.

Only later on did I realise these cheers were in celebration. They knew they'd won. The season was over.

Each year, a team of Sherpa known as the Icefall Doctors, employed by the Sagarmatha Pollution Control Committee (SPCC), are responsible for creating and maintaining the route through the Khumbu Icefall. Until the route was repaired, the climbers could not continue with their rotations. The remainder of the fixed ropes to the summit were still not in place, though the minister had ordered them to re-open it.

Henry called a team meeting that afternoon, but I knew what was coming. We all did. The defeated look on his face spoke for itself. Two of the Icefall Doctors had come to see him and apologise. They too had been threatened. Without the route's repair, every card had been played. We were one of the last teams standing, but now we were left with little choice other than to leave without even setting foot on the mountain we had gazed at the whole week, and dreamt about for much longer.

Around the tent, some of the strongest on the team welled up in tears. I wasn't far behind, either.

Others sat with gritted teeth, but we all nodded. Outside, Roman walked around the tents alone. His smile had always lit up the camp, but now he was crying. It touched my heart when he later signed my diary, "Live the life you love, love the life you live." Our final night wasn't quite as uplifting as his outlook. Hefty barrels were loaded to the brim with five weeks' worth of snacks and chocolate for our rotations and post-summit celebrations. It was no time for celebrating, but we devoured them anyway, counting our blessings that our team wasn't in the Icefall during the avalanche. We'd had the makings of an unforgettable trip, and nobody could take away the memories, even when base camp disintegrated into packed-up tents and broken dreams.

When Paul, the French climber, failed to turn up for dinner that night, we were instantly concerned. For the next thirty minutes or so, the nearby tents were scoured to check he was safe, until he was eventually found chatting and sipping tea nearby.

"What is wrong?" he asked innocently.

Considering we had only just met, the way that everyone had sprung into action, grabbing radios and head torches, spoke volumes about the bond we had formed.

We would be going home to our families. Sixteen innocent people were not so lucky.

25th APRIL 2014

We saw quiet despair on the faces of Dorje, Pasang, and the others. Whether the new reforms were positive or not, they were left worrying for their future, perhaps feeling responsible and embarrassed, even though it wasn't their fault. But as we shook their hands, there was no animosity. They had lost more than anyone.

As the yaks were loaded with our kitbags to head down, only three teams remained to climb. Before I left, I stopped to shake Henry's hand. He was visibly agitated for both us and his staff. I clambered over a rise to visit my friend Jeff Smith on the HimEx team, who would soon follow suit. Our promise to share the world's highest high-five was little more than wishful thinking now. Shoulder to shoulder, we patted each other on the back and struggled for words. Through his efforts, Jeff had fundraised over fifty thousand pounds for the charity Teenage Cancer Trust. His success was another huge positive to shine in the face of disaster, but he still had every right to feel cheated.

"I'll be back."

The base camp trails were at rush hour and blaring with heat. Everest peeked over the horizon with one final, taunting glimpse to mock us. I couldn't help but feel we weren't meant to be here. At the same time, this must have happened for a reason. I pondered hard what this could be as I stormed down the trail to Pangboche alone. Maybe the reason was our preservation, if nothing else, as painful news emerged that an Adventure Consultants cook had been killed by freak lightning on the trail near Lukla. I was never religious, but there was no denying the mountain had a spirit. We weren't welcome this year; that was certain. The mountain gods seemed mightily ticked off. And they weren't done yet.

Our agent Iswari called at Kyangjuma and told us to get a move on or we'd miss the last flight for a week, so our leisurely three day trek became a mad dash. We arrived at Lukla late that night. Torrential rain and fierce thunderstorms settled over the valley with a feeling of doom. Along the way, we passed several mani walls—religious stones inscribed with the mantra "om mani padme hum"—which traditionally you should pass on the left. Believing it couldn't get much worse, I walked to the right side of them in almost deliberate protest. I was probably asking for trouble.

I was learning the reality of high-altitude mountaineering, but being stopped by a short-sighted political power grab made the situation feel like a waste. The only positive was that it had brought global awareness to the plight of the people living in Nepal, and long-needed reforms for the Sherpas that the government had ignored. The Sherpa community had insisted the conflict was between them and the government, and the antagonists only saw one way to make change, hitting the government where it hurt most: their pockets. Every year, the Nepali government received over three million dollars in permit fees from Everest expeditions. Little, if any, reached the people in the Khumbu valley. If they could hijack this sum, they could play the government like a game. Their frustration was completely understandable, but realistically, they didn't need an avalanche. The second tragedy of the season wasn't the climbers going home, but that the antagonists bit the hand that fed them and created another problem altogether.

Most Sherpa were paid as usual by their expeditions, but from the teahouse owner down to the local farmers, everyone in the valley was going to lose out from the actions of a few. There were no winners. Many worried for the future and their jobs, wondering whether the expeditions would return to spend money and continue raising awareness for their plights, or fundraising for their kids to go to school. Sixteen lives had been forgotten in a web of lies, and although their loss had been used as a vehicle for change, it had been achieved in the most malicious of ways.

Kathmandu brought us relative comfort—if five weeks too early. There was little to do but mope in coffee shops and internet cafes. We had been hounded by the media for weeks and I refused to speak to them until now. It was going to be a tedious wait for a flight home, but Roman had his usual zest for life.

"You can have seven days bored out of your mind, or seven days to have fun!" he said.

Fun was the last thing on my mind. I would still enjoy the traditional expedition weight loss as I quickly came under with salmonella poisoning. Whilst the team drank away their tension in the Kathmandu bars, I survived on lattes and milkshakes, and spent many hours sightseeing the bottom of the toilet in my budget hotel. I refused to spend an extra penny on what had become the most expensive base camp trek in history, apart from a cheese sandwich for a homeless man on the street.

Meanwhile, two of my teammates, Chris and Scott, decided to ride motorbikes from Kathmandu to Singapore, mostly for the hell of it. As I lay sick as a dog in the dreary pit of a hotel room, I began to see inspiration everywhere. Possibilities began to spring from my mind; there was unfinished business here. The game wasn't over until I quit playing.

CHAPTER 22

Stretching Heads

"Success is not final, failure is not fatal: it is the courage to continue that counts."—Winston Churchill

Back home, my positive thoughts gave way to the post-expedition blues, a mixture of frustration, uncertainty, and lack of motivation. Instead of championing the way and proving to young people what they were capable of, I felt kicked in the teeth. What matters, of course, is how we react to the kick. But if karma didn't get me, then life would. I felt foolish for even trying to defy convention. Fortunately the salmonella confined me to bed for almost a week, so I had to keep my head down.

Most of my friends didn't know what to say to me and were equally gutted. I removed myself from social media to avoid inflicting negative energy on others, and to get away from people saying "the mountain will always be there," which became a pet-hate. Of course the mountain would always be there. So would the moon. The opportunity to be an astronaut may not be. I was young with plenty of time, but some of my teammates would never get the chance to return.

After fifteen months of dedication, I had failed to antic-ipate that something could go so wrong. This was my biggest rejection yet. Letting go of my Everest ambition would mean that I really wasn't capable of achieving anything I put my mind to. It would ruin my confidence when I had finally found my way to make a stand.

On the trek out of base camp, I had impulsively sat down near Tengboche Monastery and dropped all five of my university offers. I wasn't sure exactly why, but it did make me feel better at the time. On reflection, I guess that once I saw my dreams incarnate in the grandeur of the Himalayas, I got carried away. Whilst adventure may hurt me, I thought, routine would surely kill me. To me, success wasn't about a flashy car, a good job, and a nice house. There was nothing wrong with these, but I had already decided what was important to me. I couldn't help but feel that so many young people studied hard for degrees, but the ladder was missing a few steps.

This left me in a quandary: whether I even wanted to climb Everest anymore. The disaster forced me to reevaluate my true motivation for the climb. I needed something besides the summit itself. I knew I could return if I wanted it badly enough, but I would have to look deep for this reason if I was to find the drive to make it happen again. Until I could find one, there was no fuel to even plan a takeoff.

The swarm of criticism for Everest climbers got under my skin. Following such tragic loss of life, one Guardian journalist was distasteful enough to label Everest climbers as necrophiliacs and the mountain a peak of hubris, her nose so stuck up that it would require a two-month expedition with supplemental oxygen to scale it. The media had a field day and presented their prized photo: a huge line of figures moving up the Lhotse Face. This line was actually mostly Sherpa making routine trips to Camp Three, and they conveniently forgot that Sherpa people have been part of high-altitude expeditions for as long as they have taken place. They also mocked the use of bottled oxygen. So, is it cheating to use air when scuba diving? To use a harness when rock climbing? To drive with a seatbelt? In the same way that athletes earn

Olympic medals, does it take anything away from the achievement or the years of dedication just because somebody else won the same medal four years earlier, and every four years thereafter? No.

Everyone is entitled to come to their own conclusions, but one should question their right to holler abuse behind computer screens when they haven't been to Nepal. The greedy Westerner stereotype did not represent the people who had given everything to be there. I for one had not been slipped a cheque by an affluent parent. It hurt to read others belittling a place that meant so much to me. Being vilified for fulfilling my dreams, and for a good cause, never failed to frustrate me, though I should have risen above it.

All I really needed was the positive comments, encouragement, and support from across the world. Record-breaking American adventurer Alison Levine told me I needed to go back whilst I had the momentum. Squash Falconer, a bubbly Everest climber from Derbyshire, had been wonderful energy in my journey and two years earlier gave me her Oakley goggles for Mont Blanc even though we'd never met. The fact she still believed that one day I would take her lucky goggles to the top of the world was a credit to her in itself. If these good spirits wouldn't give up on me, I wouldn't give up either, for them or the American teenager who emailed to say my blog had inspired him to start mountaineering, the teenage son of a Twitter follower who had been shamed into going for a climb by my updates, or the young cancer survivor who now wanted to trek to Everest base camp. The list went on. My friend Richard was even planning a climb of Mont Blanc for his thirtieth birthday and citing me as his inspiration.

Whilst lying in bed I began to compile all of my thoughts into a list. An email from my personal trainer, Ian, stood out to me the most.

Subject: Looking forward to the future

Hi Alex,

I've taken a long time thinking about what to say following what's happened in the last couple of weeks. You must take solace in the knowledge that everything that you were in control of was very successful. All that you achieved up to base camp has not been taken away because of the events that unfolded.

I feel, as hard as it may seem, in the immediate future you must turn your sights away from the disappointment and channel it in another direction. You will come across many more disappointments in your time. I believe you should utilise your current fitness into a new challenge. One which doesn't have any external barriers. One that will be simply down to your drive and ability to achieve the goal. A lot of people have gone through the journey with you, invested money, charity, etc. Coming back and succeeding following adversity would give something back to them. For it is not how you achieve, but how you react from adversity that shows character.

It will take some time to come to terms with the last few weeks, and mull everything over, but you must see everything as a stepping stone developing you further as a person and an adventurer.

It rang true, but even if I had found a reason to climb Mount Everest, I needed reassurance that I was still suffering for something worthwhile, not just carrying on because that was the easiest option.

Everyone needs maintenance now and again. That was the original plan after Everest. Wasting time made me restless, but no time spent thinking is wasted time. Sitting on a bus to Chester, I dared to imagine myself on top of the world once again, accepting that I might have to settle for something less, when something remarkable happened. Goosebumps suddenly prickled up my arms. I recognised the emotions. In the midst of summer I couldn't be cold. No, the hairs standing on end could only mean one thing: The euphoria was still there. I found my happy place, and that was all I needed to know. I beamed all the way home and grabbed my diary. Putting pen to paper and dumping my ideas into mind-maps brought me a huge amount of joy. Most of the sheets ended up in the recycling bin—I already told you I'm not creative—but giving myself a new focus soon brought it back.

Within two weeks of being home, I had signed the publishing agreement for the title currently in your hands. Only now could I truly appreciate that every obstacle really is an opportunity in disguise. Each obstacle was becoming another chapter in my book. I've always marvelled at how refusing to quit can bring us opportunities when we least expect them. Knowing this and remembering how close I came to quitting before makes giving up difficult for me. As the obstacles grow bigger, my desire to conquer them grows, too. When the mountain decides that it's my time, it will taste all the sweeter.

PART 5

RESILIENCE

CHAPTER 23

Obstacles into Opportunities

"To hell with circumstances; I create opportunities."
—*Bruce Lee*

Finding my feet again was tough. The phrase "the harder I work, the luckier I get" had been my mantra until now. But what *is* luck? Whilst hard work may bring us closer to our dreams, I'd yet to witness anyone work as hard as the Sherpa people who had been dealt the worst cards of all. Ian hit the nail on the head. I needed to shake off the thoughts that something was out to get me, too.

To return to Everest, I'd have to raise funds all over again. There is no refund when the money has already been spent on supplies and permits, and it was no wonder my bank account was looking pretty sorry. Trying to find motivation was hard since I didn't have a flight booked and a date to work towards. The salmonella left me nine pounds lighter, but my mind was still heavy and unfit for decisions. Getting back to my email inbox was deflating. Here we go again. The prospect of another year of it was daunting, and I felt guilty that I'd spent so much on broken promises. I hoped a job would cover a large chunk of the expedition costs this time round, so I started applying for proper part-time work. In mid-May we should have been high on the mountain; instead I was distributing lawn-mowing fliers and half-heartedly sending out my CV.

As I tried to work out my action plan, I felt the tension building at home. Family support was one of my biggest assets that I had to protect. Luckily, I didn't need to argue that returning was investing in my future, and my family still supported my efforts even though things had gone wrong before.

Two bad seasons of negative media coverage were another challenge, if such a thing as bad PR exists. My priority was to keep my current sponsors on board rather than going back to square one. To attract new corporate sponsors, I needed to add marketing value beyond the expedition and keep the momentum building right up to Everest. If a similar drama unfolded, the sponsors would benefit anyway. Not only would it keep me motivated, but I missed the buzz of completing a challenge.

Bouncing ideas off friends and researching online gave me further inspiration. My notes came together as a series of eight endurance challenges, and "Challenge8" seemed to ring nicely. Most of the feats would be completed solo, so there were fewer logistical pains, and only I could let myself down. I kept the criteria broad, but searched for epic twists to keep things exciting. It was becoming harder to explore new places, so it was more about doing things differently. I noticed in the outdoor world that many adventurers were trying to fit in and follow a cult, which entirely defeated the point of why I challenged myself in the first place.

I had also learnt from the expeditions that it wasn't just about training hard, but training in the right way. Mental strength wasn't just about being tough or not giving up. I needed to train like you'd tune an engine, and an engine is only as good as the driver behind the wheel. Pushing through my breaking point on the bike or in the mountains would be invaluable. If I couldn't manage a twenty-hour day at sea level, I certainly wouldn't manage one at eight thousand metres. The challenges were designed to be extremely hard without overshooting, so I put each idea past Mum: if she didn't turn pale or threaten to break my legs, they weren't hard enough.

The project would support the Himalayan Trust UK, a small charity working in the Everest region for the basic needs of the Sherpa people. Being part of their culture was a privilege, and I felt compelled to do something for the avalanche victims and their families left behind. My charity target this time had been one pound per foot of Everest—29,029 pounds. I fell short, raising five thousand pounds for CLIC Sargent UK and REACT (Red Endangered Animal Connection Trust). Businesses had donated thousands, neighbours had organised cake sales, and one torchbearer friend raised four hundred pounds in a charity netball match, so the summit didn't matter as much. Even though I didn't reach the summit, the expedition had funded over 108 hours of nurses' time for children suffering from cancer, and a tree-planting session with schoolchildren in Borneo. I have never and would never spend a penny of the charity proceeds on trip costs, so I had to focus on raising these funds through corporate sponsorship, otherwise the expedition wouldn't happen and the charities would lose out even more. Next time I would have to think differently to hit the target.

I received two job offers as a charity fundraising officer from out of the blue, and getting paid to raise money sounded like the bee's knees. Choosing which one wasn't an easy decision, and I escaped for a long day to scramble in the Glyderau mountains of Snowdonia and clear my head. Eventually I made my mind up, unaware I had chosen one of two short straws. I then compartmentalised my other problems into three main areas: How can I fund Everest? How can I make this challenge series happen? Which side of Everest do I climb?

If I didn't already have enough to worry about, there was the concern of future political reprisals in Nepal. Another blighted season was a real threat, and nobody could offer solid assurances that the region would remain calm. Within the first month, other expedition teams announced trips to the Nepalese side rather than the Chinese route and said confidently that the drama of 2014 would not recur. To get an idea of team numbers, Tim had already asked me on a scale of one to ten how likely it was that I would return in 2015. I said nine. Tim had dropped the price, which made things a whole lot easier, but still, a paper round wasn't going to raise over twenty thousand pounds.

With this in mind, the Challenge8 was a huge gamble. I ran the risk of taking away crucial funds and time, and causing a last minute deficit for Everest. Many people told me the same thing. Confident in my vision, I then met a local businessman and entrepreneur, Steve Fives, in a local coffee shop, where he went for the idea straight away. He was a professional man in his forties, and he was the joint chairman of The Westgrove Group, a cleaning and security solutions firm based in nearby Warrington. I had approached him the previous summer for sponsorship, and although he wasn't in a position to help, he had been one of the first to stand after my talk at the Chester Business Club. Steve was giving his time to help numerous individuals succeed by mentoring them and I was humbled that he wanted to work with me. He reviewed the concept with great enthusiasm, when he could get a word in edgewise, and I still remember him saying, "You take care of the peaks, and I'll help you with the troughs." There would be plenty of both. It was the start of something great.

Meanwhile, being the sole fundraising officer of a charity and hitting the monthly fundraising target to earn my wage was like herding cats, even before Everest was added to the mix. Recurring depression overwhelmed me, and although I gave it my best shot, I called it a day less than two weeks later.

I soon got a job at the MacDonald Portal Hotel. It was a short-term means to pay my keep and fund the Challenge8 so all the sponsorship money could go to Everest. Time was worth twice the weight of money, and I didn't have time to look for something else. Meanwhile, I met with Textlocal to salvage what I could. Corporate sponsorship was what I knew best, and as they say, if it ain't broke, don't fix it. The directors were just glad to see me safe, but I couldn't help feeling embarrassed. Being able to set the Challenge8 concept on the boardroom table was my best chance of swinging things in my favour. I also went to London to meet Harry, the project manager at Quintessential, who thought the concept was clever. I waited anxiously for the decision makers to bite, but it gave me time to build other bridges just in case.

CHAPTER 24

The Epic Seven

"There is no such thing as work-life balance. Everything worth fighting for unbalances your life."—Alain de Botton

One of my contacts at an outdoor magazine sent out a desperate email to find someone to take over the advertising, and I volunteered, once again thinking it would be easy money. When would I learn? Securing sponsorship had become second nature, or so I thought. Finding the balance to train, work, plan the new challenges, and send sponsorship emails became increasingly taxing. There was no balance. I was getting little done. I was happy to work, but not with the bigger picture out of sight, compromising my ambitions. The twelve-hour shifts on my feet, cycling home at 1:00 a.m., and rising five hours later to cycle back started to take a huge toll on my body. It showed when I was paid to speak at a high school awards ceremony and totally blew it. Ste joked it was because of the attractive girl sitting next to me, but I was so tired I barely knew the day of the week. I was utterly exhausted. I developed a calf injury and tried to call a physiotherapist before I caused any damage, but I couldn't pronounce a single word without stammering and launched the phone into the wall in frustration. Hopefully I had remembered to hang up first.

I was lost for words when the managing director of Textlocal called to explain they weren't able to commit any financial support for round two. I shed a tear at losing a key player in my support circle. There were no hard feelings though, only immense gratitude. Fortunately, Steve and the Westgrove team had already taken a big step into that ever-growing circle. My first visit to Westgrove headquarters had started with a bang as I slammed my hand in a car door, and after several minutes of lying like a pansy on the office floor, stood up and shared my story with their team in the board-room. I did something right, as Steve and the directors en-rolled me as the company's first ever Young Ambassador. Representing the values of a business through my journey was no mean feat, and I practically bounced out of Steve's house that afternoon. Westgrove became my first head spon-sor of Everest 2015, and only then did Everest really feel pos-sible again.

Steve's wife, Jenny, was their brand and events manager, and unlike me, a diligent organiser. When Steve told me that I would become a CEO of a company before I was thirty-five,

Alex with the Westgrove team. Mentor Steve Fives, Joint Chairman Simon Whittle, and Claire McKinley-Smith

I laughed and said the company would go under. Through the mentoring sessions I received at their home, their business experience rubbed off on me and lifted the project to a new level, revealing perspectives I had overlooked. It was important to focus on the key aspect of my story—the adversity angle—to appeal to the corporate market. As we crafted the concept, "Challenge8" shrank to seven challenges and adopted the name "EPIC7" instead. I was chuffed to announce it to the world after giving my other sponsors the chance to come on board first.

Failing immediately would defeat the purpose, so the first EPIC7 challenge was straightforward. I would cycle the Fred Whitton, known as the toughest cycling sportive in the UK, crossing 112 miles over the highest passes of the Lake District with over twelve thousand feet of height gain in one day. I had barely trained for it. With only a rucksack of Soreen malt loaf, I started out alone from the town of Windermere in a torrential summer rain. Tour de Drowned Rat seemed more like it.

For nine hours I cycled through beautiful valleys and tackled forbidding inclines, my legs burning and sweat stinging my eyes as tourists sipped tea from roadside cafes. No sportive would be complete without the Hardknott Pass, the steepest road in the UK with a thirty percent gradient. Stop pedalling and you roll backwards, and there's no getting back on. I lost my balance, cut my knee, and bent my handlebars. Blood dripped down my leg for the next thirty miles. Then I realised I had taken a wrong turn to the village of Coniston instead. Somehow I found the strength to race an extra twelve miles before slumping on a bench just four minutes before the final train. The trains home were then cancelled, leaving me stranded at Crewe station with a drugged-up nutcase boasting about the fake "Who Dares Wins" tattoo on his leg. He insisted we stick together, but I ran off to a taxi rank when he started throwing punches in the Virgin Trains office.

I made it back home at 2:00 a.m., and with my mojo re-suscitated. Whether the challenges were epic or not, each would involve unforeseen drama. Ownership of the outcome was liberating; only I could let myself down. This was exactly what I needed.

The next challenge was just a couple of weeks later. I would go solo on the Welsh Three Thousands, walking the fourteen highest mountains in North Wales and ascending twelve thousand feet over just thirty-two miles. Most people took two or three days, but I would complete it in twenty-four hours.

I left the Pen-y-Pass hostel at about 3:00 a.m. to reach the summit of Mount Snowdon. As I scrambled down the arête of Crib Goch, I tried to calculate the time for each section. Time had been my weakness on Baruntse. Descending the Amphu Labsa pass was excruciating especially with insufficient food and water, and Francis had to lie and say we were almost there to convince me to finish. Sir Ranulph Fiennes once wrote how worrying about cut-off time, the time at which you must turn around on summit day to descend safely, had contributed to both his unsuccessful Everest attempts. After studying his wife's career as an equine endurance competitor, he realised that horses had to keep going over long distances whilst exhausted and with no idea when they might finish. With this in mind, I pretended to be a horse. It worked.

The path from Glyder Fach was non-existent, so I scrambled down the Bristly Ridge. The next slog up Pen yr Ole Wen loomed ahead, the low ebb when most people retired. Not me. As the sun set on Foel Fras, the final peak, I even began to run at mile twenty-nine as the Iron Maiden song "Trooper" played on my iPod. You couldn't make it up.

After eighteen hours and fifty minutes, I punched the air and collapsed into awaiting transport in Abergwengregyn village. Number two was in the bag. I stunk up the car on the way home. Mum just looked at me.

In the magazine job, I had sold enough advertising to get it to print and help my friend, but not enough to earn anything myself. Then I pitched another failed fundraiser, a fair stall for which I baked over 150 scones that even jam couldn't hold together. Thanks to Westgrove, there was no need for it, and I could afford to leave the hotel after eight weeks. It was a reward in itself when Brian Johnson, the lead singer of AC/DC, my favourite band, had stayed at the hotel.

"It's him!" squealed Chris the sous chef, coming into the kitchen pale as a ghost. The manager could fire me for all I cared (and I told him so), but I wasn't leaving until I met my hero.

Brian was one of the kindest celebrities I have ever met, besides the lovely Olympic cyclist Victoria Pendleton, and definitely the shortest.

"Bloody 'ell... yer a big'un fer nineteen aren't ya son?" he chuckled in a thick Geordie accent, posing for a photo in his trademark flat cap. I was cycling home the next day when a Ferrari 458 Italia roared past me and pulled over along the road.

"Ayup son!" cheered Brian. He recognised me and asked me for directions to the hotel. I nearly fell off the bike.

It wasn't the only time either, as challenge number three involved cycling 880 miles almost entirely solo from Chester to Chamonix in the French Alps in just seven days. No matter how much I plan, things always seem to go wrong.

I didn't even know what a headset bearing was, until it was found mine was cracked when I took my bike to the mechanic. So began a frantic mission to locate another. Dad couriered a new one from London just days before I was due to start. Working on logistics until the early hours of August 26th, I hit the grey zone again.

Later that morning, family, friends, sponsors, and mentors came to Chester Town Hall along with various local media. Also present were the Lord Mayor of Chester, the giant fluffy Chester FC mascot rabbit, and a bus full of Japanese tourists. The send-off couldn't have been more random if we tried.

The Lord Mayor rang the claxon, and I cycled the 125 steady miles to Stratford-upon-Avon drama free. On day two, I finally had the chance to meet Becky Bellworthy, who joined me for the final thirty miles into Portsmouth. I almost lost my head to a lowering railway barrier, but met my friend Giles at the door 127 miles later.

Day three took me eighty miles along the coast to Newhaven, but I abandoned the route on my Garmin after I was repeatedly directed across farmers' fields and forest trails. At the end of my rope, I was interrupted by a young girl as I stamped my bike to the ground in rage.

"Err... hi... I'm lost," I muttered, breaking the awkward silence.

Having to check Google Maps on my iPhone at every turn slowed me down.

"*Mate, it doesn't matter about the route. Just keep heading south,*" Chris had texted.

I'd just keep heading south, hauling ten kilos of gear in panniers on a bike that wasn't even built to carry them. After all, I wasn't lost. I was exploring.

CHAPTER 25

Mr. Bean's Holiday

"If an idea is at first not completely absurd, then there is no hope for it."—Albert Einstein

I felt strong as I disembarked in Dieppe at 4:00 a.m., but as I cruised along the Avenue Verte into the darkness, I felt that something wasn't right. I hadn't slept a wink on the ferry, and now I was veering off the road into the grass. Energy gels, daylight, and even a double espresso failed to cure it. Sleep deprivation is frightening. Rolling landscapes, sleepy villages, roads smooth as marble, and a lack of aggressive motorists lulled me to sleep until I cycled into several ditches, fortunately avoiding injury.

"I've had enough. It's getting dangerous," I declared as I rang home hours later. Mum had heard it before.

"Oh come on, even you know you're not giving up."

She was right. Power-napping on a bench for thirty minutes was enough to wake me up. At 103 miles, I called it a day at Compiegne to catch up on sleep in a roadside hotel. Each day became a battle against time, and I had little chance to enjoy the beautiful countryside as I raced through villages under the blaring sun. I still have those hideous tan lines today.

My eyes began to flutter on day four, thirty miles away from Auxerre. Not again, I thought. I began to recite *Monty Python* movie sketches to divert myself, but there was nobody to hear my incoherent slurs about juniper bushes and the Messiah. 136 miles later at 1:30 a.m., the night porter at the hotel waved a stale baguette at me as I retrieved a hearty dinner from a vending machine: a Snickers bar and a bag of M&M's.

Once you fall behind, getting ahead becomes incredibly difficult. I felt dizzy, nauseous, and sluggish on day six. I'd lost the sensation in my little finger because of the handlebar vibrations. The thought of riding another 140 miles that day was overwhelming. Determined not to add an eighth day, I consulted with my cyclist neighbour Richard, who persuaded me to wait. I had fuelled myself with little other than bread and sugary pastries from the boulangeries. I reluctantly retired to a hotel after forty-four miles.

Ste and Chris bared the brunt of my technology frustrations, as they had taken over my social media so I could focus on the challenge. The support I received from my followers encouraged me to keep pedalling. Engaging people had been my aim all along, and getting people reading my blog and feeling like they were with me was amazing. The thought of arriving in Chamonix carried me past the endless sunflower fields on day seven. After 118 miles, I arrived early at the Ibis in Lons-le-Saunier to find the hotel reception and the restaurant next door closed. By a stroke of luck, I met an RAF engineer who drove me into town for a Turkish kebab. His kindness saved the final day of the challenge.

On the final day I had opted last minute to head further south, which would add twenty miles but circumvent the gargantuan alpine climbs. I was unaware this route still involved over ten thousand feet of ascent. The scent of log fires from the villages and the chill in the valley reminded me of the Himalayas. After mistakenly going onto the major Auto-Route motorway and dragging my bike across a farmer's back garden, I was relieved to arrive in the Geneva city centre eighty miles later. I was dazzled by the shop windows until my front wheel jammed in a tram track and threw me hard onto the pavement beside some amused tourists. I felt like an extra from the film *Mr. Bean's Holiday* as two police officers helped me up.

Having run out of food, water, and phone battery by 11:00 p.m., I was pushing myself to the limit. At the top of a poorly lit road of chalets, the map tried to direct me down a mountain—until a sign further on caught my attention. "Warning—forbidden access to public—unexploded mines in the area," it read. Brilliant.

To my relief, I found the route down, or so I thought. After a brilliant downhill ride, I realised I'd just cycled *down* the hill I'd spent thirty minutes cycling up. Back up I went, but this time, I lost my balance and clipped a rock. I hit the road and sobbed like never before. I wanted to curl up and sleep in the undergrowth with the squirrels. But nobody would hear, or come and help. After eight days, I didn't really have a choice but to peel myself off the freezing tarmac. My family, sponsors, and friends were waiting for news of my success. There was no better way to test my grit than getting back up, and by now, I knew I had it in me.

I finally found the correct road, where a large sign read "Barree close." Road closed.

Sod this, I thought, and carried the bike through the road works, past the diggers and cement mixers, to find a great downhill leading all the way into the village of Les Houches. In the glow of streetlights, the sign appeared a couple of miles later, and I found the energy to smile. "Chamonix Mont-Blanc."

I started to laugh. Nothing mattered now. I was broken, but I'd gained a better understanding of how far I could push myself. When I didn't have a clue what I was doing, I just kept heading south. That was adventure in the truest form.

Arriving in Chamonix

Barring the drunken tourists staggering out of bars, there was little fanfare for my arrival at 2:20 a.m., 146 miles later. My stepdad's cousin Julie cheered and threw her arms around me. I took a couple of days rest in Julie's flat to ease my fluttering heart and to regain the half-a-stone in weight I had shed. Only then did I question why a residential street in France had an English sign about explosives in the middle of the road. The tricks of the mind can be quite fascinating.

My friend Paul and I then headed up to the Aiguille du Midi above Chamonix and set up camp for a few nights to climb a handful of alpine classics; back to the basics and the simple joy of being in the mountains. My life had changed beyond recognition in the two years since I'd climbed Mont Blanc, and being able to just get out and tick routes with a friend was a real milestone for me. Descending Mont Blanc du Tacul, I stumbled and felt a shooting pain in my groin. Moving up to the cable car was excruciating—I had picked up a moderate hip flexor strain, and just in time for challenge number four.

Climbing the Dom de Mischabel was epic. It was the highest peak in Switzerland and the greatest vertical ascent in the Alps. The Matterhorn nearby had been my original plan, but I decided against it because of the crowds. I knew Everest was busy too, but Everest meant more to me.

Guide James Thacker and I set off across the border to Switzerland—until I realised I had forgotten my passport. Randa was an eccentric village that reminded me of Alpen cereal, milkmaids, and mountain goats. We gained nearly a mile of vertical ascent hiking to the Domhutte through the forests. Every step sent searing pain through my hips, but if I slowed down too much, the challenge would be over. I hadn't come this far for that. I distracted myself with my iPod and recollected some grit.

We made the hut in good time and set out together at 3:00 a.m. The exposed arête of the Festigrat was mostly ours, besides a few German climbers cursing "Scheisse!" as one dropped his helmet down the ridge. Otherwise, it was still and magical.

With the stabs of fire in my crotch, a pulsing altitude headache, fatigue, and a second 1,600 metres of ascent still to go, things were getting uncomfortable. I kept my head down. The pain would stop soon enough.

James led the way up the final slope, which opened up onto the summit of Dom at 4,545 metres. White alpine peaks poked through the clouds, a picture-perfect vista that was worth the pain. I wondered how entrancing the view on top of Everest would be.

Number four was in the bag once we'd descended two miles to safety. I was soon back in Chamonix and walking with a Michael Jackson "Thriller" limp. The Dom hadn't pushed my comfort zone as I had hoped, but making decisions about my injury and bringing attention to my subpar rope work were positive steps towards Everest.

When a young man recognised me on the street and said my journey had inspired him to achieve his goals, it made it all the better. After such heights, though, the influx of congratulations couldn't lift me from the subsequent adrenalin crash. My poor budgeting meant I also ran out of money, with just fifty-four cents to eat in probably the most extortionate town in the Alps. This is why I think everyone should go on an expedition, even if only once—you no longer think twice about walking home when you miss the bus or going hungry, and you'll never complain about the weather, broadband speed, or cold showers again. You might inspire someone else, too.

I could have supported myself back home on the sponsorship money, but complacency was dangerous, especially when the Nepal Ministry of Tourism went back and forth on whether our expedition permits, worth ten thousand dollars, would be honoured in 2015 as they had agreed. I started working at The Boot Inn again, but this time as a commis chef, which was more my style. I worked weekends because separation from my inbox during the week was becoming detrimental.

Two weeks of adventure was enough for now, but when I announced EPIC7 challenge number five, "Are you off your trolley?" was one of the first responses I received. It made me smile. I was clearly onto something. I loved it when people looked at me like I was losing it. It wasn't called EPIC7 for nothing.

CHAPTER 26

I'm Gonna Be 500 Miles

"The comfort zone is a beautiful place—but nothing grows there."—Unknown

For the fifth challenge, I would cycle unsupported between the National Three Peaks in three days. Adventurer Mark Beaumont and his book about cycling the world had inspired me; and a few adventurers, including my friend Russell, had completed it the previous year and given me loads of advice. It had never been done at the end of October, though, and watching the leaves fall from the trees left me feeling dark.

Announcing the challenges one after another gave me flexibility—I just had to find the courage to do it. My friends seemed as concerned as me. Luckily, Ste wasn't just there for the fair weather, and he became my motivator. When most people might have told me to get a grip, he never shied away from helping me through the problems of each challenge. With his patience and objectivity, I often relied on his input to find confidence in some of my biggest decisions.

Soon enough, I was racing up Snowdon at midnight. I shook off the rain at the Pen-y-Pass youth hostel before jumping on the bike to cycle 160 miles to Ambleside. I made fast progress on the flat roads through Liverpool with a Garmin Edge sat-nav device I'd borrowed, a real lifesaver.

My groin injury was no longer a problem thanks to some sports massage—an uncomfortable experience, to say the least.

Darkness fell near Kendal as I moved along a poorly lit dual carriageway. A small mound of vegetation spilling on-to the road caught my eye and I veered to avoid it. Too late. The tyres lost traction as I clipped a cat-eye, jackknifed the handlebars, and flew off, my helmet whacking the tarmac at about twenty miles per hour. I was stunned. I can't remem-ber whether I was knocked out; I only recall dragging my bike and broken pannier bags from the road. Nobody stopped to help. I slumped against the railings, unscathed besides several cuts, torn clothing, and a bruised ego. I got odd looks at the Ambleside youth hostel. I was badly shaken.

I knew better than to make rash decisions, but when I awoke at 6:30 a.m. and cursed—I should have left three hours ago—I rolled over to go back to sleep. But I couldn't. Ste reminded me how Bear Grylls fell into a crevasse on his Everest attempt: he too was shaken, but carried on. Being flexible was crucial when climbing Everest. Again, I had little choice but to peel the bed sheets from my bloodied knee and pack. I cycled to Seathwaite, legged it up to Styhead Tarn, and was back in the game. In good time I summited Scafell Pike. This time I'd invested in a GPS tracker for safety, a great idea in principle, until family and friends called me in a panic. The tracker showed me going the wrong way back towards Snowdon, and when it stopped, they thought I'd drowned in Derwentwater. I was safely back in the Borrow-dale youth hostel, collecting my parcel of dried fruit and snacks, now six hours behind schedule. Cycling one hundred miles was no longer an option since I refused to touch an-other major road in the dark. The roaring fire was too tempt-ing, and I couldn't shake my fears from the previous day.

Now the challenge was to not give up. Still, the disap-pointment ground me down. I had to weigh the consequenc-es of each option and remind myself that calling it a day would gain me nothing. It was like leaving the South Col on

Everest for the summit bid. Breaking each section into five-mile bits rather than thinking three days ahead was easier to work with. I arrived at a Carlisle bed and breakfast at 11:00 p.m., where I bought sandwiches from a petrol station and met up with Chris, who had driven three hours to give me a much-needed morale boost.

"Is anything going to stop you?" he asked, smiling and carrying the bike inside.

I didn't dare answer.

My legs recovered quickly on day three, but I gritted my teeth as wagons careered past on busy roads. I'd preached about facing fears head-on to thousands of people; now was the time to practice it myself. On rough-hewn roads into the borderland of Scotland, my tyres were punctured four times. It was late and all the shops were closed. I pushed the bike along the dark road and cursed myself. Now I was really at my wits end. What the hell would I do?

A couple hours later, Chris's friend Rich Whitehouse, a former Royal Engineer, drove from Motherwell to give me some new inner tubes. I was able to make it to a Travelodge in Dumbarton, racing through the tranquil Glasgow city centre whilst most people were tucked up in bed. The next day, my body started to seize up on the unforgiving A82 to Fort William, and I could only hope the bike held together for the next ninety miles. A brutal headwind across Rannoch Moor made each mile excruciating.

"Shut up, legs!" I shouted at myself. But within a day, it would be over, and a day was nothing.

Belting out the Proclaimers number "I'm Gonna Be 500 Miles" in my best Scottish accent lifted my spirits, but in the rainy wilderness of Glencoe, I wouldn't be falling down at a girl's door anytime soon. The clerk at the reception of the Glen Nevis youth hostel looked a little surprised to see me, to say the least. The dry clothes I'd posted ahead saved me from hypothermia as I hurtled up the tourist path with a couple of Snickers bars in my pocket. Running through the wind and rain whilst singing full blast to the Red Hot Chili Peppers and hallucinating from exhaustion was the closest I'd ever get to taking drugs. The beam of the head torch was barely visible, so I began marking the route with fluorescent orange energy gels to avoid a wrong turn that might send me down Five Finger Gully, or the three-thousand-foot drop down the north face. Talk about living on the edge. At 10:00 p.m. I stumbled into the summit cairn of Ben Nevis, and the Three Peaks Cycle Challenge was complete. Better in four days than not at all.

I was so elated I forgot to take a photo with my sponsor banner. My family watched online at the squiggle on the GPS tracker screen as I wandered around in the wind. I lost the path.

"Stop. Calm. Focus," I told myself. "Don't mess it up now. You've got this." I retraced the map and navigated to safety, then waddled inside the youth hostel at 1:30 a.m. An indescribable wave of satisfaction swept over me. It took both arms to get up the stairs, and you can only imagine my dismay the following morning when the train conductor wouldn't accept my credit card to buy porridge and coffee.

More bizarre, I grabbed a photo with the Labour party leader, Ed Miliband, at the train station. A couple of hours later, my work colleagues whinged about hangovers and lack of sleep whilst I was keeled over and shivering against the kitchen wall. I usually hated lie-ins but slept until 11:00 a.m. the next day.

My nerves got no vacation as I was the guest speaker for a lavish charity fundraising dinner at the RAF club in London soon after. I ran through the usual routine: waking up with butterflies, going on a bike ride to clear my mind, arriving early, relaxing, then going for a walk to psyche myself up. I told myself that everyone wanted to hear what I had to say, whether true or not; if I didn't believe I had a good story to tell, then I'd be done. I had no idea what would happen until I stood up and changed the first slide, but I refused to sit down until I'd finished. I composed myself, and for the next thirty minutes my stammer was gone.

I'd often speak at smaller talks of less than ten people, but I presented awards to more than four hundred people at the high school sports ceremony. It had never really dawned on me how significant it was to be the guest of honour and hand out awards to others when I was only nineteen. At a primary school I spoke to over two hundred students who had drawn posters of their ambitions for me to judge, and afterwards a nine-year-old student emailed me his plans to run and swim to Germany for a cancer charity. Who's to say he won't do it? He'd even started swimming lessons. That, in a nutshell, is why I speak, no matter how much it scares me.

Working in the kitchen was less gratifying.

"What are you going to do when you stop pissing about with charities?" my colleagues said. It really got under my skin, but I was never one to argue. Fundraising, planning the challenges, and training took up the same hours, if not more, but I wasn't allowed to call it a job because I was pursuing my dream.

"Climbing these mountains pays you, does it?" they asked.

Actually, motivational speaking did, as I came home one day to find Hector the dog running around with a 250 pound cheque in his mouth. Speaking was a service, just like getting paid to cook food or drive a bus, and I was building demand.

My colleagues and I got on well most of the time, and the banter was fun to pass the time. We had a hoot. They were just good and honest people who seemed to hate their jobs enough to bring me down, too. Perhaps we are intimidated by others who live differently than us. The more I went to Scotland, the more people I met who had given up their day jobs, emptied their savings, and gone exploring in the mountains once they had figured out their lives. Hopefully unearthing my purpose early on would prevent me from having to reverse direction thirty years later. But as I'd learnt, we're all thrown into unfavourable situations, and we can either moan about them or change them.

CHAPTER 27

Red and Blue

"We are all in the gutter, but some of us are looking at the stars."—Oscar Wilde

Life was like one big triathlon: speaking in the morning, training at the gym, moving on to a photo shoot, changing into a suit on a park bench, eating a tub of rice before a business meeting, and finishing off at work with raw chunks of pheasant stuck underneath my fingernails.

It was a little insulting when my colleagues asked if I'd had trouble getting out of bed. On Saturday nights, I slept on the sofa so I didn't wake Mum up with my alarm when I left to walk eighteen miles. Physically this wasn't demanding, but carrying over forty-five pounds in my rucksack was. The misty light in the forest helped soothe my discomfort, at least until I got home with ten minutes to spare to rush to work. Sometimes I cycled eighty miles instead of the walk. This routine was doing me no good, and walking became agonising once I strained the plantar fascia ligament in my foot. If they hadn't been so short-staffed, they'd probably have sacked me for hobbling in late all the time.

Once again, my general training was prescribed by Ian and Mitch. My workload was reduced, my diet was being measured to the gram—eating three thousand calories even on rest days—and my disordered eating was finally back on track. A typical meal was rarely more exotic than brown rice, olive oil, broccoli, and roasted chicken. Food was fuel for my engine, and putting diesel in a petrol engine would only break it. You'd think that doing six minutes of reps on the leg press machine with one hundred kilograms would break it too, but I quite enjoyed it. Pumped up guys in tank tops observed in amusement as I shuddered under the effort. I liked how they had no idea what I was heading off to do.

On my regular forty-mile bike route, I passed the offices of a business called Dayinsure, practically next door to my old school. I did my research, and soon enough I was meeting the chairman. They came on board as another large sponsor, getting exclusive media coverage in return, and my sponsorship deficit was rapidly closing. Steve Fives had been speaking about me at length at various networking events, and true to his word, he had brought in other organisations as sponsors. It certainly took the strain off me. His vision was to help me form complimentary partnerships with companies to build my adventure career long term, rather than commoditised sponsor relationships. The previous year I had taken anything I could get, but I could afford to be selective this time.

I learned this the hard way. The contact for one previous sponsor met me an hour late in the staff dining room, yawned twice, tried to forge a deal worth ten-times too much, and later on asked me, "Adversity? You mean like the stutter?" Safe to say, I terminated that agreement. Sometimes the hardest thing in leadership is saying no.

Like the year earlier, the secondary networking was most fruitful. Simon Gerrard at the Cheshire FA, a friend of Steve's, had connected us to Active Cheshire. We met Anne Boyd, the CEO, for lunch. Anne was an influential member of the county, eager to be involved, and pushed hard to make things happen. When Active Cheshire came on board as the second major sponsor of the expedition, I couldn't believe my luck. It took me a while to believe it, but seeing their logo

Active Archie, Steve Fives, Alex, and Anne Boyd
of Active Cheshire

over my gear, website, and interviews made it real. As the leader in physical activity across my county, Active Cheshire aimed to get fifty thousand people more active, more often by 2017, and they would invest in me as their new Active Lifestyle Ambassador to help them market the campaign. It made perfect sense. The outdoors had changed my life and I knew it could do the same for others. We were also introduced to British Cycling, and soon enough I was speaking about my cycling exploits to nearly one hundred attendees at their team building day. This was exactly what Steve had wanted. Our mood in the car afterwards was ecstatic.

The speech I gave at a business lunch was deeply moving to the audience. One man was almost in tears afterwards. Another audience member came up to me and said she'd never complain about life again. The world seemed very small at times, as I found another sponsor in a local businessman, Mark, who had rowed the Atlantic.

Just before Christmas, I did the math, as usual, and my eyes widened in disbelief. I was going back to Everest. I couldn't have asked for a better Christmas present, although I was back at the gym on Boxing Day to get back to work. Unsurprisingly I had the place to myself.

Even though I'd cycled over 1,600 miles in the past six months, even a routine forty-mile ride soon had me swearing for motivation. I couldn't understand at first, but I realised that now the trip was going to happen for certain; I simply wasn't used to things going so well. Easing up the pressure on the challenge would lessen my productivity. I continued to think that something was due to go wrong. I went for a walk with Chris to disperse the dark thoughts, and in the local shop he asked me to point out the red and blue items on the shelf. I was puzzled.

"See? That's red!" he joked, poking a box of Malteser chocolates.

"And this! Tell me what colour this is!" I shuffled to the side.

"That's red, too!" he said, pointing at a box of crackers. A mother nearby nervously moved her young child away. But the message was clear. When your mind forecasts something bad, you watch out for it even more. I almost needed to have a problem, even if it meant creating one. I should have been a happy camper. Maybe the trauma of last time was still hanging over me, but I knew there was little point worrying about something I couldn't change. I decided to focus on everything positive that I could.

Sure, the Everest pioneers didn't have Garmin watches or gyms—so we should wear hob-nail boots and woolly jumpers because they did, too. Whilst squats in the gym were useful, no amount of squats could damage my legs, build my skills, or strain my mind as much as being in the mountains. I hadn't gotten enough winter training the previous year, and I couldn't let that happen twice. The EPIC7 had highlighted my strengths and weaknesses, mostly mental, and now was the time to practice. I was learning through the EPIC7 that Everest would only be ten percent physical and ninety percent mental. I needed to get quality training in Scotland. It takes a day to get there and back, however, and my kitchen work got in the way of travel. I got to Everest last time by being bold and I needed to do it again.

My boss had always looked after me and I hated letting anyone down. Fortunately, he was supportive.

"You need to follow your dream and move on with your career, lad," he told me. "You're welcome back anytime."

I was a bit scared at the idea of living off sponsorship money and speaking. I guess I feared I'd have nothing to do, but instead of feeling like a burden, it gave me a chance to start raising money for charity, get myself ready, and sweat the assets for the sponsors. Putting Everest first was liberating. This was a once-in-a-lifetime experience, or at least it should be, and I didn't want to go back a third time.

Before I could make it to Scotland, I went under with a viral infection. Something had dripped out of my nose that was most definitely the wrong colour. I was going to have to get used to pushing on when I felt terrible, so I left as planned for the West Highlands with my friend Adam. Near Fort William, a loch-side town that I knew well, we began climbing the spur of Sgurr a Mhaim. Spindrift tickled our ankles and the wind reddened our cheeks. It would be the first of many rewarding days in the mountains, and for me, the fun was only just beginning.

CHAPTER 28

Run to the Hills

"The mountains are calling and I must go."—John Muir

Once again, the Glen Nevis youth hostel was my hub for the winter training. Getting there wasn't easy. I tried to catch a coach at the Manchester city centre at 4:00 a.m., where a few drunken louts tried to pick a fight with me despite the two climbing axes protruding from my rucksack. Fortunately I was able to spend a combined total of four weeks in the mountains to get more experience under my belt.

All it took was a huge overnight thaw to turn the snow into grass, and I had little choice but to struggle through. Low clouds had obscured my target, until the hillside narrowed into a ridge and led me to the summit of Mullach nan Coirean.

Being the only one atop the plateau was sublime. I was in no hurry to head back down the east ridge. The silence was broken only by my raspy breath and sneezing. I could have closed my eyes and pretended I was on a Himalayan ridge. I had the headache to go with it, too. After camping at Glen Nevis, I trudged back through the Steall Gorge.

My plans to climb the munros Binnean Beag and Binnein Mor fell foul after my numerous failed attempts to cross the river in waist deep snow to reach the western slopes. Still, every day out brought me closer to my goal.

I then went to the town of Aviemore in the Cairngorms. I felt nostalgic returning there and especially meeting Matthew Dieumegard-Thornton, the young Everest climber who had inspired me three years earlier. We headed out for a few days of mixed ice and snow climbing in Coire an't-Sneachda, a large corrie like no other. The cold froze the snot to my chin as Matt confidently lead-climbed the routes and I followed behind. Sudden wind shunted us forward and we had to abandon the Fiacaill Ridge before we were blown back down.

Last year I struggled to enjoy winter climbing. Scratching around for placements whilst hollering over the wind to your climbing partner wasn't everyone's cup of Earl Grey. But for me, I started to find that being out in the elements was an opportunity to reflect on what I'd accomplished.

Two weeks later I found respite back home, although I still had general training. It was time for a rest before the final instalment of the EPIC7, but the deliberations to decide the actual challenge dragged on for weeks. It was Ste who talked me out of ideas that pushed the boundaries too far. I worried there would be no climax to fit the "epic" criteria, but that was inevitable. Seriously injuring myself would have been catastrophic. There was always a risk, but in 2014 someone had broken an ankle walking around Everest base camp. It was a balancing act of risk and reward.

At seventy-nine miles, the Great Glen Way is a long-distance footpath from Fort William to Inverness, without the treacherous ground like the West Highland Way where I might twist an ankle. I aimed to complete it in two-or-so days. It was the distance of three marathons, and I would complete it in winter weather. It was a different sort of challenge altogether, but with just six weeks before the trip, I had nothing to prove. After a night in a hostel in Fort William, I couldn't wait to get going with just my rucksack of supplies. Deserted paths took me along Loch Lochy, and after several miles I began to hobble again—my Plantar Fascia injury had come back with a vengeance. I didn't have much choice but to continue to the nearest road, which happened to be in Fort Augustus, my destination. Thirty-five miles later, I arrived an hour earlier than scheduled. This was a first for me.

At the hostel I found myself surrounded by bearded men playing banjos and violins. Things got even weirder when I arrived at an esoteric gathering of hippies the next day. My legs were remarkably fresh, but the difficulty lay in being alone for long periods of time with the pain in my foot. I would soon be able to rest it. Until then, I distracted myself with the scenery and navigating, and put my watch away to avoid checking how far I still had to go. On Everest, by comparison, I would be distracting myself by keeping warm, monitoring my oxygen levels, and clipping into ropes. The Great Glen was training my mind to switch off from the bad things and switch on to the important.

Walking beside the waters and through the forests in solitude was quite a treat, though. At this moment, I was right where I wanted to be, a mere speck on the hills above Loch Ness. The Loch Ness Monster didn't show its face, but I couldn't help gazing through the morning mist at the vast expanse of water and pondering the mysteries of its depths. Maybe I just needed to get out more, but doing challenges released me from the burden of my social anxiety.

I would have been able to push on another twenty miles from Drumnadrochit to Inverness if not for my foot. I opted for an early start instead. The hostel was ancient, and as I made porridge at 4:00 a.m. the next day, I half expected the eighteenth-century photos on the wall to spring towards me like something from the *Paranormal Activity* films. The street lights faded once I made it up into a dense forest of skeletal tree trunks, engulfing me in eerie darkness. I've never understood why we are so afraid of dark woodlands and how this is engrained into our psychology. As I pushed up the path at double my average pace, my phone bleeped with a photo message from the horror movie *The Exorcist*. Chris had seen the stellar opportunity for a chuckle.

By daylight, Inverness was merely four miles away, but that still felt a long way off. Those final miles were a tedious slog. My ankles ached with every step. I arrived in Inverness for lunchtime, having covered seventy-nine miles without any of the drama that had plagued the rest of the EPIC7. I was relieved—I had finally learnt something about planning. Now all I had to worry about was Everest.

I wasn't finished up north, though. Over the coming weeks, Scotland threw everything it had left at me. With my friend Mick, I added the Ballachulish Horseshoe to my repertoire, taking in three major peaks close to the shores of Loch Linnhe, near Fort William. We were descending unroped when I saw a large rock tumbling down the slope, leaving a crater in the snow just a metre behind me. The impact would have sent me down like Jack and Jill. It was sobering to say the least.

Not long after, and closer to home, my photographer buddy Giles and I went out to Snowdonia National Park. I had forgotten my tent, but another friend lent me his, which I pitched in a seemingly sheltered dip on a hillside in the Ogwen valley. Out of nowhere snow flurries swept down the mountain Pen yr Ole Wen and pummeled us. I felt increasingly vulnerable. Giles' beard was full of icicles. The wind was blowing our rucksacks away until we ice-axed them to the ground. As things got more serious, we stuffed the tent inside the bag and legged it downhill to camp behind a farmer's wall.

"Get the stove on!" I called over the wind, fumbling with the guy-ropes outside.

At about 11:30 p.m., I crawled inside and enjoyed a hot chocolate and a high-five from Giles. It was the outdoors at its best.

CHAPTER 29

Carpe Diem

"Give a man a fish and you feed him for a day; teach a man to fish and you feed him for a lifetime."—Maimonides

I tried to enjoy the home comforts before I left, but the anticipation was enthralling. My training could be tapered down, but life was a whirlwind that didn't let up.

For months I had been working with a local production company called Veracity Digital on a short trailer film about my journey, whilst various radio stations wanted to interview me over the phone. I always blamed the phone signal for the stammer, but the station had to cut me off live on air with hundreds of thousands listening in. I felt responsible and wanted to provide a return for my sponsors in case I didn't get them the summit photo this time round either.

Some media opportunities were easier, like cycling on a glorious March morning. Sir Chris Bonington, the president of the Himalayan Trust UK, had agreed to meet me for a promotional photo that I could use in the media to encourage donations. I couldn't believe he had just walked in. He was a cheerful and pleasant fellow, and very sorry to hurry off, but I was speechless as he wished me the very best of luck. When I thought it couldn't get any better, his assistant invited me into the office for a coffee, a real privilege that had me buzzing all the way home.

I met an organisation in Liverpool, World Merit, a global platform connecting young people to opportunities for making positive change in their communities. I hoped that as an ambassador I could help raise awareness about their work. I wanted to do more, and I was still torn about choosing a second charity to support through Everest. It seemed too big an opportunity to not support something a little closer to home, but I needed something that connected with my story. Active Cheshire came up with the best proposition, suggesting I start a fund to support adversity. Setting up my own charity was another goal of mine, but the process was long and I didn't have time. Active Cheshire, however, could receive the donations and allocate them into a specific fund, from which I would choose where the money went. I refused to name it after myself to begin with, but I eventually gave in. Money raised for the Alex Staniforth Adversity Fund, split with the Himalayan Trust, would fund projects in the region that supported young people facing adversity by helping them to live a more active lifestyle. It would be the first time I hadn't fundraised for wildlife conservation, but creating a legacy in my home community was too good an opportunity to miss.

We raised thousands of pounds at the Cheshire West Sports Awards, where I also had my biggest speaking presentation yet on behalf of Active Cheshire. The event fell on Friday the thirteenth. I was afraid, but I tempered my fear. It was similar to the Chester Business Club talk I had given almost a year earlier. Once again there were a few dignitaries in the room, not limited to the Lord Lieutenant of Cheshire, Sir Philip Craven (who opened the Paralympic Games in 2012), and three of my main sponsors. No pressure.

I knew the score, and I stepped into the spotlight to find that, sure enough, my slide presentation wasn't working. I thought back to the person who had stood up the previous year. As the AV technician tried to fix it, I told jokes to pass the time and mocked his song collection. It was the best performance I had ever given. For those twenty minutes, I was a whole new person. I walked back to my table to the applause as someone tapped me on the shoulder.

"Alex! Look!"

I looked up and gasped. It was an even bigger standing ovation. All two hundred people around me were on their feet clapping. Steve texted me immediately from the far table; he was almost running out of superlatives.

It seemed life couldn't get much better, until we finally learnt that our expedition permits would indeed be extended for the 2015 trip—providing we coughed up an extra 1,150 dollars within the next two weeks. Various contacts and sponsors chipped in and quickly covered the difference. Sometimes the biggest problems are the easiest to deal with. I would leave nothing else to chance this time, though.

I had enough time left to walk the Snowdon Horseshoe, a popular scramble in Snowdonia, with my good friend Ste. It was hard to believe that just a couple of years prior, he had been trying to coerce me back to the village of Elterwater after we'd hauled forty-pound rucksacks uphill and camped above Angle Tarn. Things were very different now. Walking along in the crisp ice in the sunshine was a real treat. I could have turned round and gone back up—it was the closest thing to a walk in the park I'd ever had in the mountains.

Weeks earlier, I had climbed my hardest route to date, a grade four ice climb on the north face of Ben Nevis. I had walked the formidable Carn Mor Dearg arête with two friends and the leader of a mountain rescue team, who was impressed. Reminiscing on everything I'd learnt assured me I could take care of myself in the mountains. At long last, it seemed like my self-doubt was gone.

The well-wishers who came to visit me before I left told me repeatedly that I *would* summit Everest. I shrugged it off. As I'd discovered the hard way, nobody could know for sure. I had even stopped thinking about the view from the top, scared of tempting fate, or perhaps because it was just unimaginable. They also told me that my challenges helped them push further during their own runs, and I was glad to have impacted their lives, however insignificantly.

The tables had turned—now people were coming to me for help with sponsorship. The critics came back too, and when one student sent me a barrage of abuse, I wrote a blog in protest and raised an extra seventy-five pounds of donations for my anti-bullying fund. I think I won. Sceptics are loud, but actions are always louder.

It seemed there was nothing left to worry about when I went to discuss the final arrangements with my sponsors at Steve's house. It was emotional to say the least. Anne from Active Cheshire had said months earlier, "Sometimes the Plan B becomes Plan A all along," and only now did I understand what she meant. Everything had come together this time round.

"See you on the other side," Jenny said, tearing up a little as she hugged me.

"Hopefully," I said with a smirk, which in hindsight probably wasn't in the best taste.

The night before I left, Mum secretly filmed me dancing around the kitchen with my dog Hector in my arms. She warned that if I hit my charity target she would make it viral.

Despite everything good that had happened, I couldn't ignore the feeling of dread in my gut. Something didn't feel right that I couldn't quite put my finger on. I said nothing. It would only worry Mum more. Quite soon, I would learn why.

CHAPTER 30

Déjà Vu

"No man ever steps in the same river twice, for it's not the same river and he's not the same man."—*Heraclitus*

28th MARCH 2015

The day was here. I had the opportunity to do something phenomenal. Perhaps this time my bedroom poster would come to life.

Our African grey parrot, Maxi, squawked "Don't be long" from her cage as I heaved my kitbags down the corridor. I wouldn't be long this time, Maxi. But home as I knew it would never feel quite the same again.

I guess I'd seen it all before. Once again, I was sewing sponsor badges onto my rucksack on the drive to Manchester Airport. I still couldn't shake off the premonition I'd had at home. Maybe the video of me dancing with Hector would be my last, something that Mum might remember me by. She wasn't the only one close to tears in the Departures Lounge. As the flight took off, I felt numb and zoned out. My energy and confidence from the past weeks were gone. After the EPIC7 and everything else I had endured, it would be bad if I couldn't stay resilient so early on.

I remembered the farewell coffee I had with Chris just days earlier. There were no last minute conundrums to work through, a sign of how far we had come. This time round he had stepped back a little, not from lack of interest, but because he hadn't seen me asking so many questions and looking for assurance. I was my own man now—or at least I had been a few days earlier.

"If you feel you need to prove yourself anymore then you're not ready. Just be. You are well prepared," he'd said. Now I had to believe it, which was easier said than done.

I was void of emotion by the time I touched down in Kathmandu and met the team for dinner in the centre of Thamel. Last time, our three-person team had conversed little. Not this time. Tim had Ellis and two other British climbers on his team. David, a sixty-year-old accountant from Yorkshire, had been on Everest with a different team the previous year. Aeneas was on his second trip to the Himalayas, but his first on Everest. He stood out as the strongest of our group. Two trekkers would also accompany us to base camp: Loraine, a bubbly nurse from the south of England; and John, a cheerful older chap who also happened to be Tim's dad. Both brought a boost of life to the trek.

"*What happened to the plane landing in the fog at Lukla? It mist!*" Ste messaged me, instantly lifting my mood as I sat in the terminal the next morning. After going through security, which was being tickled by the "x-ray hands" of a uniformed man, I somehow lost the "Live the Dream" bracelet that my grandma had given me as a good luck charm. I chalked it up to coincidence. We landed on the miniscule airstrip the next day with ease, excited for what lay ahead.

Our tried and tested itinerary was almost identical to 2014, so the beginning of our trek along the bustling Khumbu trail brought no surprises. I could never grow bored meandering through the sweeping valleys with the Himalayan peaks towering behind them. Each day changed like pages in a travel brochure. I breathed in the warm fresh air like incense, beyond grateful. The camaraderie of trekking flooded back, too. We drank sugary tea together, played hours of card games, and warmed up in teahouses under smelly blankets at night. Tim was even still slightly obsessed with tomato egg drop soup and corsani.

I had left my own appetite at home. Eating teahouse food on previous expeditions had made eating a chore and no longer a pleasure. David had the right idea by dousing everything in marmite. Back home I was a porridge connoisseur, but out here the porridge looked a bit too much like baby food. Even the muesli caught my throat. I was used to following a regimented diet plan, so when Tim offered the team a bottle of Sprite, I got cracking looks for asking for boiled eggs instead.

The subsequent improvements in my strength, cardiovascular fitness, and mind-set were quickly apparent. "Slowly, slowly catchy monkey," was my mantra, but I think I'd already caught him. As I'd learnt from the EPIC7, I just needed to be a horse.

Hydration was an art, but I made every effort to drink enough, although worried how my body would cope on summit day without the water it had been trained to perform with. At least this time I was worrying about the important things.

It was easy to forget exactly why I was here as I passed the time daydreaming and chatting with our local guide, Dep Kumar. It was the perfect time to bond with the team. I got along well with Aeneas, who was easygoing and had a good sense of humour. The hike to Namche Bazaar was hard for everyone, but especially the porter in sandals who silently followed us with a one hundred kilogram load of plywood strapped to his back. Further up, a British girl, also nineteen, struck up a conversation with us, assuming we were going to base camp.

"We're staying there, yes," Aeneas replied with his usual reservation.

"How come you're here till June then?" she asked.

We smiled and looked at each other.

I laughed. "We might as well just say... We're going to the top."

"Wow!" she said, firing away with questions as we walked up to the village. My stammer had disappeared. She wished us luck as we parted, and it all went a little quiet.

"Are you gay?" Aeneas asked in disbelief. "You didn't even ask her name!"

By my standards, it was hardly surprising. I smothered my incompetence with a slice of chocolate cake at the Everest Bakery. We were at 3,400 metres. I had bigger fish to fry at that moment.

Even if I didn't know exactly what was coming each day, I could look forward to things like visiting Tashi and Lakpa again. They were equally excited to see us. When I could get a word in edgewise, I told Tashi about my fundraising for the Himalayan Trust UK. She told me of a young family nearby who couldn't afford the lodging for their six-year-old daughter, Jyoti, to attend school. I agreed straight away to pay the cost, about 580 pounds a year—a child's education should not have a price tag. Those who visit Nepal are so touched that they want to leave it better than they found it. Nothing

The wonderful Tashi Sherpa at Ama Dablam Lodge.

can speak more to the warmth and graciousness of the Nepali people.

Another cordial welcome awaited us in the village of Maralung. Ang Chutin, whom we had met the year earlier, was away in Germany, but her father Phurba, who had climbed Everest a whopping seven times, greeted us just as warmly. It seemed Phurba had enjoyed a bumper crop of potatoes as we were lavished with complementary plates of the boiled delicacies. Stuffing my face did little to motivate me. I was struggling for momentum already.

The year earlier I had been fine, but this was how it worked sometimes. Even though I'd been drinking enough water to shower a vegetable garden, I felt rotten and reached for the paracetamol. The descent from the pass to Gokyo was quick, but I was exhausted and retching. Every hundred metres or so I leaned onto my trekking pole and closed my eyes, hoping for a slight breeze.

"Relax and breathe, Alex, take your time, it'll all be fine," I repeated in my head.

My adventurer friend Squash Falconer had told me this before I left. I also remembered the Three Peaks Cycle challenge and began to break down the route into sections. I would aim for a rock poking out of the snow, maybe two hundred metres away, permit myself a sip of water, then repeat until I arrived at the lodge. When I did, the thought of Rara Noodle soup turned me pale as snow.

At the Fitzroy Inn, Tenzing and his brother remembered me straight away and ushered me inside their spacious dining room. We chatted about his plans to visit the Lake District as they brought food and coffee, yet Tenzing continually shook his head when I offered to pay. They had so little but gave so much. To think that thousands of trekkers must stay in their lodge each year, I was flattered. It's a great feeling to know that I'll always have friends whenever I return to Gokyo. I remembered Gokyo's charm well, especially how violently your head throbbed if you went too quickly up the stairs.

As we descended into the sleepy Phortse village, I was reunited with another friend: oxygen-rich air. We finally got a glimpse of Ama Dablam, Lhotse, and Everest.

"There's our girl," I marveled. "What am I doing here?" also sprung to mind.

We were only at four thousand metres. Everest's summit stood at 8,848 metres, but she finally felt touchable. Rumour got around that the route through the Icefall to Camp Two had already been fixed, so there was no reason to feel otherwise. I was more ready than I had ever been.

CHAPTER 31

—◆—

Worlds Apart

"Be who you are and say what you feel, because those that mind don't matter, and those that matter, don't mind."—Dr. Seuss

As we trekked on, we were having our cake and eating it, quite literally, at the Hermann Bakery of Pangboche. I missed contacting home, but I revelled in taking each day at a time, and wondered whether I was missing something since David was already preoccupied with the finer details of summit day. He even asked Tim at what point he could tell we had the required stamina to summit. He said he already knew there would be no problems, which was reassuring. I had the stamina to ascend Chukkung Ri peak, our highest elevation so far, and reaching the top in good shape boosted my confidence.

We didn't have much to do in the afternoons besides relaxing in teahouses. Loraine practiced Qigong meditation outside, and even had the porters mimicking the movements. Unfortunately, not everyone in the team shared her positive energy.

"So why haven't you got a career?" someone asked. Here we go again. I thanked him for the concern and confidently explained my life plan.

"So how much money do you owe your sponsors?" he asked next.

He wasn't the only one to pipe up—apparently young climbers like me were thought of as uncontrollable, lacking the strength of mind to match their strong legs. I finished the game of cards, furious, and walked up the hill to sit beside the crumbling stupa shrine and think. Looking down on the village below the Taboche peak was soothing.

"Calm the hell down, Alex. The guy pays for his thirty-year-old son to come on expeditions," I told myself.

However my teammates judged me, I did not have the typical commoditised sponsorship relationship. I was not handed a cheque and waved on my way, as nice as that might have been. Nor did they know about the corporate experience, mentors, and network I had developed through my training. This year my sponsors and I were even friends on Facebook! They had become like friends outside of the business world.

Get a job? *This was my job.* If I could diversify, there was no reason why telling the story of adventures couldn't be sustainable income. Maybe they were right. Either way, you have to feel sorry for anyone who feels righteous enough to judge another person's situation—whilst also claiming to hate asking people for money. My life plan, monthly income, or reason for not being in school was none of their business to begin with. It certainly wasn't important right now. I couldn't speak for the rest, but I was here to climb Mount Everest and get back down again. Nothing else mattered.

Even though I received condescending comments for the remainder of the trip, I ignored them. I had earned my right to be here like everyone else, and all I expected was to be treated the same, not to feel unwelcome on the team. I tried to distance myself from them on the trail the next day even though it meant going too fast. Ahead of the group, I bumped into the unmistakable figure of Henry Todd and his client, Tom, near Chukhung village.

"Hey man!" he said in his Edinburgh accent, stopping for a brief chat and pointing out the snot hanging from my nose.

"Slow down—you're out of breath. Behave!" he added.

I nodded. With Henry, I always did as I was told.

Compromising myself to prove a point was stupid. With five weeks ahead of me, I had to brush the conflict aside the next morning. This was made easier by the heavy blanket of snow we received overnight. For the welfare of our porters, Tim abandoned our ascent of the Kongma La pass and diverted us over the Dughla pass, where we saw hordes of base camp trekkers sparsely equipped and wearing basketball shoes and tracksuit bottoms.

The crown of the mountain pass held the memorials for the victims of Everest. I had seen them before, though the plaques had never had such a profound effect on me. One was particularly heartbreaking, the memorial for a German doctor who had "Lived his dream, died on the way down." I had felt confident and comfortable with facing the risks, yet nothing could extinguish that bravado like remembering the lives lost on the mountain.

Near base camp there were more memorials imprinted onto a boulder, as a sly voice from behind pointed out.

"You don't want to end up on one of those!" he said. I ignored him. Of course I bloody didn't want to. My family meant more to me than the mountain, and being victimised was just winding me up.

Base camp was a welcome sight. The fresh snowfall was warming, emotionally at least, and there were handshakes and hugs all round as many of the Nepali staff had returned from 2014 with their usual smiles. As we unpacked into our new home and shook off the glacier dust, it felt like we'd only just left a week ago. The crunch of ice beneath my feet had never felt sweeter. There was no political agenda to taint the peaks or the breathtaking array of stars in the night sky. In fact, the only foul smell came from the flimsy toilet tent—

and my sleeping bag, as I'd had difficulties peeing into a bottle.

The cook staff warmed up each day well before the sun. "Helloooo good morning! Breakfast ready!" they would sing, fetching trays of omelettes, hot cornflakes, and fresh chapatti from the kitchen tent. I placed myself near the end of the table so I could get to the leftovers easily, but I think everybody knew what I was doing. Fortunately, there were familiar faces in the mess tent to share it with. I was thrilled to see Ellis Stewart back again after a second massive fundraising effort, and he looked even stronger than last time. Dr. Rob Casserley and his wife MK had also returned for another attempt, as had Dan Wallace from London, and my Icelandic friend, Ingo. We were joined by Rolfe Oostra and his client, Jo Bradshaw. Rolfe was a prolific and decorated mountaineer who fit the bill with his scraggy dark hair, black bandana, and Berghaus attire. Jo was an experienced expedition guide herself and chatty, whilst Rolfe observed and laughed often. We got along well. Her evident toughness boded well for

(Left side, from front) David, Rolfe, Aeneas, MK, Jo (Right side, from front) Loraine, Tom, Ellis, Tim, Alex, Ingo

their plans to climb Lhotse, the world's fourth-highest mountain. Tom Martienssen was the closest to my age at twenty-four, and I liked him, too. With untidy hair and more civilian clothing, he looked a touch misplaced, but he had served in Afghanistan for the Royal Air Force and could clearly endure. He was now a journalist working for BBC World News, but we rarely saw him out of his communications tent, where he posted reports about base camp life and the stories of the climbers. Tom was not aiming for the summit—he had been told not to climb above base camp, probably in case anything went wrong again.

We said our farewells to Loraine, as nobody is allowed to stay at base camp without an expedition permit. Unfortunately, Tim's dad John had turned around days earlier.

My well-wishers back home were pressing for our proposed summit date. We had no idea, and even if we did, I wouldn't announce anything until the right moment. I was careful with the updates I sent home from the 3G spot near camp. Ingo had marked the precise spot on the glacier with the word "welcome." The line of sight down the valley to Gorak Shep village gave intermittent internet access to anyone prepared to stand around shimmying to stay warm.

"I don't know if you realise, but we have a *really* strong team," he told me one morning. I felt the same. Ingo was laid back and like a brother to me on both expeditions, forever teasing me for saying I had no time for a girlfriend. I did often worry he was more interested in girls than the summit. Back in Kathmandu he had bought a tray of Sambuca shots for a party of British girls in a bar under my name, but I made a quick escape and foiled his attempts to fix me up.

Our sirdar, Kame, wouldn't send any Sherpas up the mountain until they'd had a Puja blessing. It appeared the logistics and camps wouldn't be in place until April 25th, which was well received. Four days was nothing in the grand scheme of things. We just needed nothing bad to happen and release the tension from last year. It also seemed respectful to wait until the anniversary of the 2014 avalanche had passed. I tagged along with Tom to the neighbouring Jagged Globe camp to attend a memorial service for the victims, led by the Gurkha200 expedition, a team of Gurkhas celebrating two hundred years of service to the Crown. The one minute silence was an unforgettable privilege. From the line of perhaps a dozen soldiers in their G200E blue jackets, one stood forward and broke the silence with the sharp din of bagpipes. Base camp clammed up. A lump caught in my throat. Afterwards I went to introduce myself to the leader, Captain Dick Gale. An ex-Gurkha friend of my family had mentioned me beforehand, and their welcome was accordingly warm. They invited me over to their camp, but I didn't feel worthy to accept their offer of Diet Coke and beer. There was nobody better to have on my side than a team of Gurkhas. They were revered as the hardest, most acclaimed military force in the world.

Our own Puja blessing was an equally humbling occasion. The ceremony was held by a Lama from a local monastery who tied blessed strings around our necks. I still wear mine today. We celebrated with laughter and cheers, followed by trays of Chang (the local spirit) and divine offerings of Snickers bars and biscuits. Being there in the moment was blissful. There were no hostile vibes, providing Ingo didn't carry out his threat to hood the Lama in his orange parka jacket.

The Sherpas had posed together for a photo afterwards, and Kame introduced each of them to us. There were cheers and claps as Tim introduced us in return. We stood just metres away from each other, but our lives were worlds apart. One of these short, unassuming men would be my personal Sherpa high on the mountain, carrying my spare oxygen and ensuring my safety. I never liked calling them "mine." I certainly didn't own anybody. They were our climbing partners, and climbing alongside them was an honour.

*The Himalayan Guides Sherpa Team. (Back row, from left)
Saila, Kumar, Bhim, Tenzing, Gyan, unknown, Padawa, Thundu, Kame (our sirdar) (Front row, from left) Pasang Temba,
unknown, unknown, Ang Kajji, Jhyabu*

*Lhakpa Thundu enjoying himself during the Puja blessing.
Dan Wallace on the rear left.*

CHAPTER 32

Premonitions

"By failing to prepare, you are preparing to fail."
—*Benjamin Franklin*

For the climbers, there was little else to do besides washing our clothes in bowls of water, reading, and enjoying regular "snack attacks," when we raided the food barrels for crackers and licorice. It wasn't as squalid as people often imagine—you just had to improvise. My first shower in three weeks involved a tent cubicle and a bucket of hot water.

After stepping outside, human again, I saw Kame and Laxman watching the Icefall intently with a radio.

"Camp One?" I asked Kame.

"Below Camp One, our boys," he replied, gesturing downwards.

Everything was going according to plan, but the only thing I could focus on was what would go wrong first. I tried to shake off the thought before I jinxed it.

We trekked up to the nearby Pumori advanced base camp, about 5,750 metres, for a few hours away from camp. You could have snapped the view from the top straight into a frame. There was no evidence of a camp up there, and finally Everest's glory was no longer obscured. Damn, did I feel lucky to be there.

We began our acclimatisation rotations in preparation for the summit push. Good technique saved time, and every second saved in the Icefall was a second less exposed to danger, so we refreshed a few rope skills over on the glacier below camp. Jumaring up—ascending a rope using a small handheld device called a jumar—and abseiling down the large ice pinnacles was good fun. In the heat radiating from the glacier carpet, I kicked my crampons into the ice and lowered myself down the slopes, aware that Tim was watching my every move.

Mostly for curiosity, Rob and MK tested our blood oxygen saturation and resting heart rate to see how well our bodies were adjusting to the altitude. I was alarmed to see my stats were the worst in the tent. I shrugged it off, but inside I felt a little cheated by the training I had put my confidence in. As I was fast learning, fitness doesn't always equate to better acclimatisation. The following day we would head into the Icefall for the first time for further acclimatisation. I tried to go slow and drink plenty, but even four litres a day didn't feel like enough. Rob tried to assure me.

"Remember Alex, you're as good as anyone else," he said as I left the tent. I nodded with a confident smile.

Only seeing the Icefall up close could I truly appreciate the terrifying labyrinth that every climber must enter to scale Everest. I had read the tales from the comfort of my bedroom, but here I couldn't turn the page to safety as I moved upwards through the massive blocks of ice scattered across the glacier. As the slopes grew sharper, the first of the fixed ropes led us beneath frozen towers that threatened to topple at any moment. Crossing the yawning crevasses on ladders was not for the fainthearted. You put your lifeline in flimsy pieces of metal and hope your crampon doesn't snag in the rungs. If not for Tim saying, "This is the real thing!" I might have struggled to believe I was really there.

As the ice groaned around me I realised how unforgiving this place could be. We were at the mercy of the landscape; it was no place to hang around in awe, however much

Alex acclimatising in the Khumbu Icefall

I wanted to. A team of IMG climbers passed us on their way down looking done in. That would likely be me soon. But for now, I was too busy enjoying the journey to worry. I felt good when we turned around at about 5,800 metres and headed back to camp.

Once the four camps were in place, we would be ready to strike when the weather allowed. Our first of three rotations would take us through the Icefall to Camp One at just over six thousand metres, where we would stay for one night before moving up to Camp Two, at 6,400 metres. We would stay there for two nights before returning to rest. On the second rotation, we would reach Camp Three, and on the third, we'd go all the way for the top. Camp Two had more supplies and even a small cook tent where Pasang Temba would prepare our meals, but moving too high too soon from base camp could be dangerous.

In the storage tent were several blue barrels overflowing with packets of dried food. We would probably take too much up the mountain the first time round, Tim said. With this in mind, I was ruthless while sorting gear in my tent, but my rucksack was still too heavy, and I dreaded carrying it in the morning. We had no choice but to stash our gear in the high camps for our next rotations, and busting a gut now was better than later on in the trip, when we'd need every bit of strength we had left.

We raced outside the mess tent as a colossal avalanche thundered down the Lho La at the far end of base camp, a twenty-thousand-foot pass that frightened climbers daily by releasing car-sized ice blocks without warning. Distant avalanches were little more than entertainment at base camp, although the timing was a little close for comfort. The tents below were safe. As far as I knew, nobody had been hit by an avalanche at base camp before. Still, it was an impressive sight.

I went to the 3G spot to send Dad a photo. I didn't mention the avalanches—he was already worried enough. I also ordered some flowers for Mum to arrive the 28th of April, exactly halfway through the trip. She would need them more than ever.

There was little left to do but wait for night to fall and drink plenty. Rolfe eased our nerves by cracking inappropriate jokes that had me laughing until my head throbbed. We all felt the apprehension and excitement as we prepared to head into the unknown for the first time.

Inevitably I tossed and turned for a few hours in my sleeping bag. Everyone else must be feeling the same, I told myself. Within hours I would witness the Western Cwm, or the "Valley of Silence" as it was once called. I tried to imagine the valley and remain calm. I had already gotten this far, and anything else was a bonus. There were no more baby steps. What could possibly go wrong now?

The answer would sweep the world from beneath my very feet.

PART 6

AVALANCHE

CHAPTER 33

Guardian Angels

"Life is inherently risky. There is only one big risk you should avoid at all costs, and that is the risk of doing nothing."—Denis Waitley

SATURDAY 25th APRIL 2015

The alarm sounded at 4:00 a.m. The Sherpas had already left earlier in the morning to carry loads to higher camps. Frozen zippers spluttered to life as our team assembled sleepily outside. Lying in my sleeping bag, I looked to my side at the photo of my dogs—my guardian angels. They would look after me. I already had my gear laid out for fear of forgetting something. I padlocked my kitbag shut since the tents would be unaccompanied for three days. As I stepped outside, my first thought was that it was a damn unpleasant morning. The gloomy clouds hung low, leaving only the lower section of the Icefall visible in the distance. Turbulent winds and snow flurries rattled the tent and the Union Jack flag I'd secured outside. Some expedition leaders had been concerned enough about the weather to postpone their plans for another day.

As I hauled my rucksack towards the mess tent, I felt the physical and psychological weight on my shoulders. I knew it would be a tough day, but I told myself it would all be over soon. I was thankful for all the Sunday mornings I'd spent heaving my forty-five pound rucksack through the forest. The morning sun barely broke through the thick, sludgy mist, but the ground was well lit. I was one of the last to enter the mess tent, sort out my gear, and fill my bottles with hot water. Nobody said much. It was early and we were too excited. Breakfast arrived from Kumar, who always smiled regardless of the hour. Everything seemed normal.

Breakfast was dry toast washed down with coffee and milk tea. We were ready to go by 5:00 a.m. As Tim led us through the ice, we passed our Puja altar without offering any rice like last time. I wondered briefly if this would matter.

Base camp was quiet as we crept past the tents of neighbouring teams, our boots crunching in the snow. Climbers marched ahead like an army of ants, their head torches twinkling on the ice. It seemed laughable that I'd been worried about the political recurrences of last season. We reached crampon point in the lower section of the Icefall, where we kitted up and moved onwards in a line. We exchanged smiles with friends from the Gurkha200 team who were passing by.

Within thirty minutes or so we'd made it to the first ropes, and I began the monotonous routine of clipping and unclipping. I couldn't find a rhythm in the jumbled terrain. I'd been fine two days earlier, but no matter how thorough the acclimatisation process, sometimes you just have bad days. The effects of altitude made my breath short and my body feel strained. Everything took more effort than usual, but I couldn't pinpoint or relieve the discomfort. Ellis was struggling too. Rob soon caught up and asked how I was doing.

"So much for being young and fit," I said.

He told me I was doing fine and to stay with Ellis, which was certainly welcome advice. Unfortunately, the remainder of my team raced ahead and was quickly out of view.

Even a handful of Jelly Babies from my pocket failed to invigorate me. No matter how slowly I trudged up the icy slopes, I found no respite—all I could do was keep going for a few hours. I knew I was capable, but that day I felt like I had never been on a mountain in my life. That was fine. I just had to keep going, all the time perilously close to the crevasses. This was just the beginning of the more technical sections still ahead, but I would worry about them when I got there. Gyan, one of our Sherpa team, appeared around the corner on his way back to base camp, almost bouncing up and down with the ropes in one hand. It was here in the mountains that his people truly excelled.

The heat was oppressive and stuck my clothes to my back. I didn't take much in as I tried to distract myself. Camp One was the target, and there was no point dwelling about days that followed. We soon made it to the first of the ladders, where we saw the Korean team that included the first blind man from the country attempting to reach the summit. Even with his team's support, I couldn't grasp how he felt, although not being able to see the Icefall was an advantage I envied.

Ellis held the ropes taut as I crossed a twenty-foot ladder over a black abyss, angled at fifty-degrees and held together by a bundle of frayed rope. His VHF radio crackled to life as Tim asked our location.

"Hang on, just let me take this," he shouted across.

I looked around in disbelief, suspended halfway up the wobbling ladder whilst they chatted for a minute or so.

"Nice one, you're closer than I thought, just keep coming up," I heard Tim say.

"Thanks Tim, over."

I looked back, bemused.

"Sorry about that," Ellis called up innocently. I chuckled and continued to climb.

Tim had waited for us further up, near some prayer flags stretched between two ice blocks the size of a house

"How long till camp?" I asked, hoping for some final momentum.

"I think it should start to level off up there, where those guys are," he said, pointing to a few figures above on the horizon.

I explained what a difficult time I was having.

"It's your first time up here carrying a heavy load. But you have to be mentally resilient," he said. He was right, but in my current state of mind it wasn't particularly encouraging.

I moved on alone for the final section. Huge blocks of ice loomed over the glacier. Sherpas and porters were abseiling down on ladders over the crevasses and snow bridges. At over 5,900 metres, my altimeter confirmed I was nearly there. I thought about the sixteen Sherpas who died near here in last year's avalanche and what a terrifying place this would be to lose your life. Slightly nauseous, I moved with my head down. The ground was increasingly flat. Each rise lifted my spirits, giving me hope that this might be the last. Thick mist still smothered the mountain, but after months of training in Scotland, it was nothing new. There was little spiritual about it, just a hard slog like any other.

Suddenly a stupendous crack shattered the silence, sickening me to my stomach. I jumped up, startled.

"Shit!" I muttered.

I knew this was the sound of ice breaking free from the mountain. A distant roar followed as an avalanche accelerated and rumbled down the west shoulder of Everest to my left. Adrenalin took over—I moved faster than I had all day as the roar grew louder and the ground began to tremble. It was coming right at me. I had little more than ten metres of visibility. I considered lowering myself into the top of a crevasse, but if the anchors were pulled loose, I would fall hundreds of feet to the bottom. I glanced left; I could just make out the low seracs and the featureless turrets of the cliffs. About a minute had passed, but time seemed to be standing still. I believed it would miss me, that I'd escaped, and felt an odd rush of calm. There was only a slight trickle of snow as I gasped for breath, disorientated.

I stopped for a moment, puzzled. Then the avalanche hit me like a snow cannon aimed at my face.

So this is how I die, I thought as the fear overwhelmed me. Visions flashed through my mind—my family's reaction to the news, the sixteen people who died last year, and my stupidity for coming here. Flung down onto my knees, I was prepared to die in the next few seconds. I would be encased in ice, never to be found. The snow blinded me and forced its way down my throat, suffocating me. I turned my head away to gasp for air. My glasses were ripped from my face and everything went blank. There was nowhere to run. I could only stand alone and face my fate.

I panicked and staggered back to my feet. Should I unclip? The rope was my only lifeline from the crevasses. I kicked and punched the air in a futile boxing match against mother nature. This would give me the best chance of airspace and therefore survival. Maybe forty seconds had passed; time had frozen.

Suddenly the snow dissipated and the mountain fell quiet. I lifted my hands to my face. I was still alive, shaking, and standing in the same place.

The next few seconds were a blur. I could feel nothing but my heart pounding. I knew another avalanche could follow. But first, I thought about Tim and Ellis. They'd been closer to the seracs; I assumed they'd been buried.

"Aeneas, David, it's Alex. We've been avalanched... send for help. Over!" I cried into the radio, my voice trembling.

No response. Shit.

I repeated again. Nothing.

"No, no!" I bawled. "Fucking Answer!"

Fearing the worst, all I could do was continue. Vomit rose in my throat. Then, looking down, I saw that the ropes had disappeared. Panic set in, until I pulled them out from the foot of fresh snow on the ground. Camp One was out of view but I moved as fast as I could, expecting to plunge through a hidden crevasse at any second and too scared to care. The radio crackled to life.

"Tim, it's Aeneas. Are you guys okay? We're a bit battered but we're okay, almost at Camp One, over."

They couldn't hear my reply. Aeneas sounded shaken up.

Seconds later, Tim answered that he and Ellis were fine. I cried with relief. All I remember Tim saying was, "It was a bit of powder,"—an understatement—and, "I can see Alex about a hundred metres ahead."

I looked around and saw a few figures in the near distance. I staggered on, staring at the ground and shivering. An orange tent appeared through the fog, an oasis on the horizon. I hugged the two trembling figures, struggling to hold back tears. I was no longer alone.

"I thought I was gone," I said.

"So did we," Aeneas said quietly. The blast had wiped the lenses clean out of his glasses. David's face was pale, his jacket covered with snow.

"We could have died," he whimpered over and over again. Aeneas almost had to shove him to camp. I'd never seen grown men in such a state.

They explained that the remaining ropes had gone. Moving further could mean plunging into a crevasse. The enormity of the situation dawned on me. The SummitClimb cook tent was metres ahead, in view and out of reach, whilst Sherpas and climbers tried to salvage what they could. We could only assume that the other tents at Camp One had been flattened. We stood still in disbelief. It looked like we would have to pull bodies from the glacier. I hadn't prepared for this. Aeneas suggested we eat something to stop the shock setting in, but the best I could manage was a few Jelly Babies.

I feared for the remainder of the team who had already reached camp until Rob and Rolfe appeared on a short-rope, equally relieved to see us all. They'd been unable to make radio contact with Tim and Ellis, who emerged shortly after, hardly saying a word. I was unable to follow their talk, too anxious to reach the tent. The tents appeared intact as we traipsed behind the rope twenty minutes later. Everyone greeted and hugged us, one by one, and my eyes swelled with tears.

The others had assumed we were dead. I discovered later that Rob and Rolfe were actually on a rescue mission for Aeneas and David. As Ellis and I were so far behind, it seemed to them that either we had not survived, or we were out of reach and would not last the night. Nobody had even been looking for me, which was hard to take. On Everest, you can't endanger your life to save someone else.

Rob radioed Henry at base camp while we listened. The relief in Henry's voice was apparent when he heard we were still alive.

"Is everything okay with you?" Rob asked nervously.

It crackled back to life. "It's total destruction... Everything's gone, chaos, it's an absolute mess..."

The floor dropped out from under me again. Others cried and cursed in denial. I should have been a wreck, but I was too stunned. Our home was gone. How could the entire valley have vanished? The words tormented me as I tried to imagine the unimaginable. This was not just an avalanche. The nightmare had just begun.

CHAPTER 34

Sitting Ducks

"In a time of destruction, create something."—Maxine Hong Kingston

We were at over six thousand metres. I was ushered inside to shelter and warmth. Aeneas shoved equipment through to me as I shakily removed my boots. Sat side by side, we contemplated what had just happened.

"You're alive and we're going to be alright, we have to focus on that," he reassured me, slapping my shoulder.

"What do you mean... earthquake?" I asked, confused.

Aeneas raised an eyebrow, shaking snow off his jacket. "Didn't you feel it?"

Exhausted and distracted by the noise, I had failed to notice the most powerful earthquake Nepal had seen for eighty years as it shook below me for over fifty seconds. The others at Camp One were waiting to die or preparing to run when it felt like the glacier was literally going to slide down into base camp. They thought the shaking had been caused by the avalanche. In such a situation everybody assumes they have witnessed the same thing. Only now could I begin processing the chain of events that led to the disaster. I would never understand it completely.

I dialled the keypad of my Thuraya satellite phone. I didn't know how Mum would react, but I owed it to her to tell it how it was.

"Hi! Are you at Camp One now?" she said excitedly.

"Listen... before you see it on the news, we've just been avalanched. But I'm okay. We're all at Camp One."

She demanded to know more. I tried to sound strong. I asked her to let everybody else know. I can't remember much else. Nothing sunk in. Her world had just turned upside down and there was nothing she could do.

"I'm not coming back to this bloody place. I'm done with Everest. I'm done," I had muttered into the handset. She was probably glad to hear it.

The rest of the team gratefully borrowed the phone in turn. I asked for it back before we ran out of credit and severed our only means of communication with our loved ones.

Shock and exhaustion made me feel like a vegetable. I could barely move the few inches to light the little Primus stove. At the decreased pressure, it seemed to take forever to melt enough snow for a drink. I was severely dehydrated, and my racing heart was cause for concern. Aeneas took care of me when he didn't have to. He was unfazed, extremely capable, and made a great tent partner. He forced me to eat, drink, and look after myself when I had given up caring.

The afternoon melted away as I eavesdropped on the frantic conversations outside, but for all I know I could have been dreaming. There was talk of moving on to the less exposed Camp Two, but this meant risking altitude sickness at the worst possible time, and sure enough, some climbers at Camp Two were already in urgent need of evacuation. Trying to get there would also be a death wish, as many of the ropes could have been broken, the crevasses closed, and new ones opened up along the way. We would sit tight for a day at least.

Camp One is vulnerable, hemmed in on both sides by Nuptse and the west shoulder of Everest. Both regularly spewed avalanches below. Indeed, years earlier, Camp One had been destroyed by an avalanche. Only a few millimetres of synthetic material stood between me and the avalanches falling every half hour from the aftershocks. It was a race against time for the 170 climbers who were trapped helplessly below.

Rob popped his head into the tent, clearly tense. "Do you know if Damian survived?"

Damian Benegas was the expedition leader moving up the ropes just behind me only a couple of hours ago. I felt sick as I suddenly remembered everyone like Damian: the teams behind us, our staff, and my friends at base camp. Would we ever see them again? Over 470 people had climbing permits this year. The images were gruesome. I couldn't imagine base camp could be gone from what sounded like the plot from a cheap horror film.

Shortly afterwards, I overheard the crackle of a radio, followed by a pained gasp.

Pasang Temba and Tenzing were dead. Kumar was on oxygen.

I stared at the pathetic tent above me in disbelief, completely numb. Their names rung in my ears.

We brought our gear inside the main vestibule in case another avalanche swept the last of our supplies away. Our rations for food and gas would only last one more night and breakfast as it was. Later on, I forced down a pack of boil-in-the-bag meatballs. The smell was nauseating, but without it, I would be depleted if we had to descend.

Tim appeared as it grew dark. Putting on a brave voice, he told us to keep the brews going and preserve our gas supplies. We could be up here for a few days, perhaps a week, and focusing on our own survival came first. His face betrayed his grief. "Then, we grieve for the people that we know later."

The next morning I could barely move. The sound of helicopters was a pleasant surprise, even though the nightmare was still fresh. The first of the climbers was evacuated after twenty-four hours cut off from the world below. Despite worries that other helicopters might never reach us in time, we thought that maybe now we stood a chance.

Once the sun rises, the Western Cwm can swing from negative twenty degrees centigrade to twenty-five degrees in a matter of minutes. The tent began to swelter and I stripped down to base layers with my gear scattered beside me.

It was then that I realised that the monstrosity had become reality. The heat scorched the tent until Aeneas evacuated himself next door for a game of cards.

As I crawled outside for the first time to collect snow, I felt like a vampire in the sunlight. Rob asked how I was doing.

"Couldn't be better," I said sarcastically, then felt bad for snapping.

I took some Diamox to alleviate my altitude sickness. I drifted between sleep and waking as the medicine coursed through my body.

The expedition leaders arranged meetings at 8:00 a.m., 12:00 p.m., and 6:00 p.m. to discuss the condition of the Icefall. Having the leadership of the Gurkhas around was a blessing without the disguise. There was talk of moving through the Icefall at night when it would be more stable.

"Did you hear that?" Aeneas asked. "If we have to go down and we're too tired, then tough shit. We have no choice."

I gulped. The thought of going anywhere near the Icefall paralysed me with fear.

A team of expedition leaders was going both up and down the Icefall to try and find out for certain. New Zealand-based Adventure Consultants had decided not to cooperate, having chartered their own helicopters to fly their climbers and gear out that morning. A few climbers booked their own independent helicopter rescues, and the hum of the rotors echoed in the valley throughout the afternoon. That afternoon, the mountain came alive again.

The ground shuddered violently and startled me awake. Everyone was scrambling. An aftershock hit, lasting about ten seconds. The glacier wobbled underneath me.

"Is that a..." I began. Zippers whizzed and everyone scattered.

"Everybody in the tents! Shut the doors!" warned Rob loud and clear.

Awaiting death was nothing new. Another monstrous roar tumbled closer towards us. We were sitting ducks. A feeble blast of snow showered the roofs of the tents, then nothing. Once again, the mountain was quiet. Maybe the next time around—it just wasn't possible to be scared for so long. Aeneas had stayed with Tim. Soon all was calm, and I continued melting snow and nibbling biscuits on my own.

The catastrophe was already making headlines. Mum sounded broken when we next spoke, her voice devoid of its usual warmth. Home seemed a million miles away. I wondered whether I would see it again, hug my family again, get married, or show the grandkids newspaper cuttings of my adventures. Someone else would be telling my story for me.

We had no idea at the time that Damian Benegas had not only survived, but risked his own life to go down through the Icefall that morning to assess and repair the route with terrible visibility. He emerged back at Camp One, having survived the aftershock, but his efforts had been destroyed. Moving over 170 people through the Icefall was not worth the risk; the purists can say what they like. Helicopters were now our only way out.

It would cost 2,500 dollars per person to helicopter down to base camp. I had no choice but to agree, and my family pressed for the same in disjointed text messages. Rob took the lead, coordinating via radio with base camp and fighting to get us out.

"Come in Bhola. It's Rob, over," I heard outside the tent. He was struggling to make contact below whilst the critically injured were evacuated. We learnt we'd leave the following morning. It barely registered. Nothing did.

I had a bittersweet view of the sun setting behind Pu-mori through the tent door. If we weren't marooned in a death zone, I might have enjoyed it. This place seemed too beautiful to be so callous. There were many innocent souls in Everest's macabre history book, and plenty of space left on the pages.

CHAPTER 35

———•———

Into Oblivion

"In all natural disasters through time, man needs to attach meaning to tragedy, no matter how random and inexplicable the event is."—Nathaniel Philbrick

MONDAY 27th APRIL 2015

Aeneas nudged me awake. "Wake up, get out of your pit," he ordered.

It was 6:43 a.m. I overheard someone say that the helicopters would come in an hour and a half. We didn't have long to get our gear ready for evacuation. Our tents were left as we'd found them, though nobody would be coming back up.

Outside, Camp One looked otherworldly. The clear skies gave us our first view of the hanging seracs that had tormented us for two days. Corrugated flutings of snow had somehow remained in the walls of Nuptse, though piles of avalanche debris were gathered at the bottom. We were microscopic compared to the mountains. Lhotse, the fourth-highest mountain in the world, dominated the head of the Western Cwm. Fissures of crevasses lined the glacier beneath, and Camp Two was hidden behind the snow blocks. It was the highest point we would reach.

Close to collapsing, I urged myself to the helicopter landing site where about twenty people had congregated on the glacier. One hundred metres had never felt so far away. Every step stung like needles. My lungs struggled to extract any oxygen from the air and my fingers turned white. I realised I'd been trying to take photos without wearing gloves until Tim scolded me.

The Manang Air AS350 Eurocopter had begun ferrying climbers down to base camp. Another group stood maybe one hundred metres away, waiting for a second helicopter operated by Simrik Air. Both helicopters were stripped down to the bare minimum in order to generate lift in the thin air, only taking two passengers per flight instead of the usual six. This would take a while.

I looked back at the Lhotse Face without trepidation, nor sadness, but in relief that I would go no further. From here, it looked excruciating and fierce. My will to climb had been swept away.

"Here we go again," I sighed to Ellis.

"I know mate," he said, sorrowful. "There's nothing more we could have done."

Icy snow blast kicked up into our faces from the chopper. Finally our turn came. Ellis and I were shoved through the door, our rucksacks thrust into our arms before the door was slammed shut. The machine shuddered and began to hover before sweeping down just metres above the ice. I could soon make out the debris and blue barrels strewn across the lower Icefall, more than five hundred metres from base camp. We had no idea what we were heading back to.

Our flight lasted no more than three minutes, undoing seven hours of painful ascent. When we were dumped on the helipad we found base camp strangely calm. It was unrecognisable. I had to sit down several times. We called by the Adventures Global team to check on a friend; a Sherpa emerged from their dining tent to tell us he was safe at the nearby village of Gorak Shep.

Only in the following days, weeks and months, maybe years, could I possibly begin to understand how an earthquake turned Everest base camp into a crash site of detritus strewn over the mountain side. We didn't like what we had learnt. The earthquake had released huge sections of ice between the high ridge of Pumori and Lingtren above. The walls that usually defended us from the elements had crumbled into a far bigger avalanche described by many like a skyscraper of snow, rock, and ice, pulverizing anything in its path. The ridge protecting base camp many hundreds of metres away should have protected it from the avalanche, but it had stormed the defences anyway. Some thought the cracking sensation was the glacier supernaturally splitting open. Poor visibility on the mountain had cloaked base camp all day and compounded the tragedy—many assumed the bellowing sound came from the Icefall as was usually the case, and were concerned for the climbers currently moving through it. It had been too late to run for cover as the avalanche swept over them at one hundred miles per hour. I thought of Pasang Temba, who was deaf. He wouldn't have stood a chance. By comparison, we had gotten a dusting at Camp One. And that had been enough.

The usual landmarks were hidden as we trudged along like the living dead. I wondered how anything could have survived. The devastation grew progressively worse. The central section of base camp, maybe a hundred metres wide, had taken the most direct hit. The Himalayan Guides camp was obliterated, and had I not followed a few of the Gurkhas, I could have walked straight past. All that remained of the cook tent were stone foundations and a few broken plastic containers. The mess tent fared no better, having been tossed a hundred feet into the air and slammed into the neighbouring camp, its once solid frame now mangled.

The impact had come at 11:56 a.m. We would likely have been inside awaiting lunch. Those inside the mess tent had sealed the door for shelter, unknowingly sealing their own fates.

Being in the arms of the mountain had been the safest place of all, I knew that much.

The Sherpas had managed to throw together a make-shift cook tent in our absence. Padawa was standing silently outside with Kame and a few others as I approached.

"I'm sorry," was all I could manage.

He nodded without saying a word. I asked Gyan if the staff were okay.

"No, no, not okay. Kumar, Pasang Temba, and Tenzing die... Bhim and Ang Kajji injury, gone to Kathmandu," he explained. I didn't know how to react.

After recuperating from illness, Kame had returned from his home in Pangboche after the quake. This illness had potentially saved his life. Henry emerged with a badly in-jured hand. He had been spared by diving behind the Puja altar, a three-foot-high block of stone. Henry had found Kumar and Tenzing in a bad way and there was little he could do. Pasang Temba had died almost instantly. The inju-ries had resembled something from a bomb blast, and Phil Crampton was tasked with wrapping their bodies. The trau-

Bhim, Kumar and Ang Kajji Sherpa at the Puja blessing.

ma would have been too much for most people, myself included, to endure. I couldn't even bear to stay in the cook tent whilst Rob stitched up Henry's wounds.

The shredded skeletons of tents and equipment were piled to one side in the snow, and equipment recovered nearby was laid out on a tarpaulin. Amongst the wreckage was the kit bag I had laid beside my sleeping bag when I departed for Camp One. Most of my gear had survived, along with a grapefruit-sized shard of rock which had penetrated the heavy-duty nylon. Such impact would have undoubtedly cracked my skull like an egg.

The team congregated atop the bank. We were in the right place. There was just nothing. The pristine snow was tainted by a few patches of yellow fabric from the tents, laid to rest many metres from where they had stood just two days earlier. Our tents lay encased in hard ice, maybe a foot deep, which made digging hard labour. Tom kicked away the snow from the level platform where his communications tent had stood. All of us had cheated certain death. There was no need to announce it.

Base camp was large enough that teams further across the valley were unscathed. Some climbers at the far side had even returned to finish their dinner once the avalanche had dissipated, unaware of the destruction and desperate rescue efforts nearby. In the Himalayan Rescue Association (HRA) tent, British doctor Rachel Tullet had saved twenty-three lives despite suffering a cracked patella. Doctors had battled through the night to keep people alive, even if they could only comfort the injured who were not going to survive.

My friend Paul Devaney from the Irish Seven Summits team, who was on his final leg of his Seven Summits challenge (to climb the highest peak on each continent), witnessed the trauma and survived to tell the tale.

"Once the energy of the earthquake and avalanche had dissipated, I headed into the middle of camp with my buddy Teo. The level of destruction became immediately apparent. The middle of base camp had been flattened. Tents in pieces, personal items and clothes embedded in the snow. We got lucky with our camp location and had just avoided the main impact. Amazingly the HRA tent survived in the middle of camp and the medical staff were already engaged on a frenzy of activity to stabilise and save those who had taken the brunt of the impact. We asked the doctor that most simple of questions... "how can we help?" He instructed us to help carry an injured man to the International Mountain Guides (IMG) camp which was half a mile away on the southern flank of base camp. The rest of the day became a series of carries to make-shift care centres at IMG, HimEx, and Asian Trekking. Most of their climbers were at Camps 1 & 2 so their tents were mostly vacant and large enough to house the steadily increasing numbers of injured and dead. The system employed was as follows... serious injuries to IMG, walking wounded to HimEx and overflow to Asian Trekking. Folks were appointed to stand at loca-

tions along the route to steer traffic. Clients and Sherpa were as one in supporting the recovery effort. Base camp had evolved into a trauma centre and many of its residents into amateur first responders. It was an astonishing scene led by some amazing people exhibiting the sort of innate courage that drove them to Everest in the first place. In those moments I was incredibly proud to be associated with them and Everest."

By now, most of the injured and deceased had been airlifted into the valley. We started to dig for lost belongings, and it was hard to know where to begin with no "X" to mark the spot; a grim treasure hunt with no treasure. Digging became exciting as we hoped to find our valuables buried beneath the ice. Our tents were slowly unearthed. Mine was only identifiable by the khata scarves I had tied to the exterior. A frozen pack of tissues was all that remained in the torn material. I imagined myself wrapped in the tent and tagged by name and team like the victims had been.

The remains of Alex's tent at base camp.

All we could do was begin the clean up—if we knew where to begin. Each whack of the axe was head-splitting. I managed maybe fifteen minutes before succumbing to exhaustion. I slumped against some containers and fell into a daze.

"If you're just going to lie around, you may as well be dead," Tim barked at me.

Until I recovered, I was little better than dead to everyone. The heat had sucked the life out of me. Jo told me to look after myself first. Quick to the mark as always, Saila brought me a cup of milk tea. He and the other Sherpa simply got on with the job they took pride in doing. It is safe to say I would not have reacted with such resilience had the roles been switched. They would always be heroes to me. Three friends had died in front of them; they could have chosen to go straight home, to whatever they had left, and nobody would have intervened.

At the time, we knew little about the other fatalities at base camp, let alone across the rest of Nepal. Word passed between us, and folks back home told us that Kathmandu was even worse off. We learnt that Jagged Globe had lost a client, Google executive Dan Fredinburg, an American who was raising funds for two Nepali orphanages through the ascent. He had suffered massive head injuries, and it was his own team members who discovered he didn't survive.

Climbers accept the risks. Failing to return home safe was not heroic, it was a waste of everything. Climbers knew this. Control had been taken from the victims in a way no one could understand. Nobody should die at base camp, either doing their jobs or living their dreams.

CHAPTER 36

Battle Scars

"Luck is a very thin wire between survival and disaster, and not many people can keep their balance on it."—Hunter S. Thompson

This was unprecedented. We searched the glacier, sifting through everything from assorted boots to bent spades. I struggled to imagine how the valley would ever heal. Sweet wrappers, bottles, and even cans of tuna had been spilled onto the ground, but the things of sentimental value like books, clothes, and even drawings, were littered about, wasted. Some rocks were stained with blood. There were shards of wood and metal, bent pots and pans, socks, down jackets, and sleeping bags. Goose feathers blew back and forth in the breeze. The carnage was just as bad closer to the Icefall. Some barrels of equipment had been flung nearly half a mile away and were now half frozen in the ground. We milled around in circles as the hours blurred into one. Jo and Rolfe had the hardest time, as their tents had been swept over the bank and were nowhere to be found.

Adventure Consultants already collected a large amount of wreckage into a massive lost and found post, including one of the boots I'd left in my tent porch. Most bizarre was an upturned table, decorated with a vase of drooping plastic flowers.

David came over and patted me on the back. "Well... the dream's over for me mate, but there's still time for you," he said. But climbing was the last thing on my mind as I pondered the terror that the victims had faced. Krishna "Kumar" Rai had been energetic and charming. Tenzing Bhote and his clueless expression made us chuckle. Both had been in their late twenties and had great potential. Pasang Temba was a veteran of twenty Everest expeditions, loved by many for his cheeky grin. All three were proud of the job that gave their children a better future, but all three were just memories now.

I kept those memories alive as I sat alone in my tent with a plate of Dahl Baht. I was too dehydrated to cry. As darkness fell, I strained to see beyond the seemingly solid black walls around me. How on earth they had salvaged new tents and made something so appetising in these circumstances was extraordinary.

People back home presumed we were safe now. I was taking no chances. The risk of another avalanche of the same scale was minimal, but every slight rumble had me shooting upright. I would take cover behind the large boulder a few metres outside, I decided, should disaster strike twice.

TUESDAY 28th APRIL 2015

I slowly regained strength but lost all motivation to move when I remembered there was little to go outside to. We were sleeping in a morgue and I wanted to get out. Henry got Tom on one of the first helicopters to Kathmandu the day earlier, although hardly any camera gear had survived to join him. Most teams had already moved down the valley. Dreamers Destination, settled just metres away from us, had barely left a trace. Those of us left turned over base camp the best we could.

I went to look underneath the pile of gutted jackets nearby. MK revealed to me that it was the body of a climber, still to be evacuated. Even as doctors, I can't imagine this ever became easy for them. It sent a chill through me that the smouldering heat of the glacier couldn't warm.

After digging a snow bank and finding only a pair of ripped trousers that afternoon, I watched as three more of my teammates were bundled inside a helicopter. The last victim—the one I had encountered earlier—was loaded alongside them. They lifted off to Lukla and would eventually be reunited with their families. I didn't have any responsibilities or anyone depending upon me, so it only felt right for me to stay and do what I could to help.

"Alex!" called a voice below.

My friend Sam, an adventurer from London on the SummitClimb team, was walking towards me. Only as we threw our arms around each other now did I realise he and his wife Alex were safe. They had been trapped at Camp One, too. I guess now we had shared an experience that few people ever would, and it was one we would never want to repeat. He told me how their leader Dan had screamed at them to get their ice axes as the avalanche hit Camp One—but they faced avalanches from all directions. Their team lost Tom Taplin, an American filmmaker who had remained at base camp that day due to fears of the Icefall danger, and had been thrown three hundred metres by the wind blast alongside his video camera.

Dreamers Destination fared even worse. Ninety percent of their team were injured and evacuated, and their other teammates had been less fortunate. Yomagato Horoshi of Japan had perished after being evacuated to Kathmandu. Zhenfang Fe from China and Renu Fotedar from Australia had been killed along with two Sherpa staff, Shiva Kumar Shrestha and Lhakpa Chhiring.

Madison Mountaineering had lost their beloved American doctor, Marisa Eve Girawong. A Vietnamese-American trekker, Vinh B. Truong, had also died. Adventure Consultants had lost five Sherpa. The youngest, Pemba, was only nineteen years old, and cheated of the future that I still had to look forward to. The blood-splattered tent I found churned my stomach.

The SPCC camp had lost two of their Icefall Doctors, which perhaps explained the cross and flowers that had been placed beneath the rock where their tents had been tossed down twenty feet. We heard reports of even more Sherpa being killed at base camp, yet there was nothing definitive. Most sources held the death toll at base camp to be twenty-two, and that was still twenty-two too many.

Hearts across the world broke as the victims' relatives learnt that they would never get to hear their loved ones' tales of adventure. When I left home, I had promised my own family that there was nothing to be worried about. What was the worst that could happen? I wondered if their families had been told the same. My eyes filled with tears when Aeneas handed me a piece of torn paper: the photo of my family and dogs, the one that had given me comfort before I'd climbed up the mountain to escape. Nothing could make me more grateful to see them again.

Most of the teams located in the central area had been on the mountain that day, including ourselves, the Gurkhas, Madison Mountaineering, Adventure Consultants, and the rest of SummitClimb. Otherwise, the number of fatalities could easily have doubled, if not tripled.

The Gurkha climbers had lost over seventy percent of their belongings. I found my sleeping bag ripped up and buried in ice, and Captain Gale was looking for his wallet. Many had been stripped of the cash and left empty amongst the debris. The looting was disappointing, since the expeditions had been trying to unite. We unearthed Tim's classic Connect Four game under a bank of snow and smiled for the first time in days. Next I saw the black tube of an oxygen mask. Through digging I found more oxygen regulators and masks, largely intact, some even brand new. Henry gave them out to most of the teams at base camp. His eyes lit up in astonishment when I brought them in.

"Oh, marvelous! You are an absolute star!" he exclaimed.

Seeing some joy in his face motivated me to excavate the whole pile. Lhakpa Thundu and the rest joined in until we found over nine thousand dollars' worth of equipment. I got a little carried away, as Aeneas pointed out to me with wide eyes. "You've gone purple!"

I panicked, but having two doctors in our team to check me over was a blessing I hadn't paid for.

Digging at that altitude all day was harder than any EPIC7 challenge, but preserving myself seemed pointless now. I didn't want to leave without doing my best to find as much as I could, not just for me, but for those on my team who had long given up. Part of me didn't care either, but there was no point standing around. It was disappointing to think that within a week or two, the snow would melt, exposing our belongings to the elements and whoever took first pickings.

WEDNESDAY 29th APRIL 2015

A fresh snow dump brought my hopes down with it. There would be no chance to find anything; the mountain had taken the treasure. As I looked around my tent, I started to notice more and more of my belongings missing. That paled in comparison with what the people of Nepal were now facing.

We packed our bags to leave. Helicopters circled above, churning up freezing spindrift all around us. Some prayer flags were draped over a large granite boulder overlooking the remains of the Himalayan Guides camp. The idea just came to me, and I took my Sharpie pen to the boulder and wrote the names of our three Sherpa teammates.

Tribute to the lost Sherpas

I gave my head torch and down-filled boots to Gyan, who had gone to extra lengths to help me. I couldn't find the words to thank Kame. The rest nodded blankly as I thanked them. Saying goodbye to the Sherpas and leaving them with such hardship hurt me. As we began the four-day trek to Lukla, I vowed that once home, I would do everything in my power to help them rebuild their lives.

My gratitude to be alive stamped out my bitterness as I glanced up at Everest. This was the first year since 1974 she had betrayed all ascents from either route. The ridges now looked insurmountable as they sliced the sky. Trying to conquer a 29,029 foot mountain was a game of chance—I had to get up and down again before she noticed and gave me a kick in the backside. Many climbers, myself included, were fearful the mountain had a sting left in her tail.

But how would I use my story to make a difference now? How could I continue this journey that had become the centre of my life and purpose? Would I ever find that joy again? None of the answers seemed to matter at the time. It was a done deal.

I knew that adversity was part of my DNA, but this was a whole new level.

CHAPTER 37

Ghost Valley

"We do not see nature with our eyes, but with our understandings and our hearts."—William Hazlitt

This was not just a disaster for Everest but for Nepal as well. The earthquake had taken over nine thousand lives and shattered many thousands more. We were just a tiny part of it.

The trails were lonely, devoid of life, and littered by stones from the crumbling walls. Most groups set to begin their excursions to base camp had turned around in their tracks, leaving the Khumbu valley unusually still, the smoke clouds of cremations rising from monasteries down the valley.

At the village of Pheriche, the damage was worse. About ninety percent of buildings had severe cracks and loose blocks on the floor, if the walls hadn't already been reduced to rubble. I was no builder, but I knew most of the homes were going to need some serious TLC. Many could have used another aftershock to flatten them completely so they could be rebuilt from scratch. Floors were gone, roof frames had buckled, and very few had escaped damage. One home was reduced to a wooden door frame, which nobody would be opening anytime soon. And how were the people going to afford the repairs when the tourism they depended upon had been wiped out? I worried for them.

A bearded man in a bright jacket flashed a camera at me as I stormed through the village. It was Reuben Tabner, a British photojournalist I was supposed to meet for an interview days earlier. He would surely excuse me for not showing up. Reuben welcomed me inside the Himalayan Rescue Association for a pot of tea.

"How's it going?" he asked.

"Could be better," I said.

"Could be worse, I'm afraid."

I didn't know how to reply, considering that days earlier his wife Katie had been dealing with the injured and dying all the way through the night as they were lifted out of base camp.

The damp fog shrouding my view was eerie and reminded me of the Icefall. Every slight boom or bang on the hillside, real or make-believe, had me jumping out of my skin. I didn't realise that the devastation of the avalanche was following me home. From a distance, I could see a huge cavity in the wall of Sonam Lodge in Pangboche village, right where we had slept.

"Going down?" asked a young boy. I nodded.

"Go safely," he smiled, waving his hand. I smiled back, and carried on down to visit Ang Chita, a young Sherpani who singlehandedly ran another teahouse in a quiet corner of the village. Tim had sponsored her children after her husband died in an avalanche on the mountain Ama Dablam, and whenever he visited, she showed her appreciation.

Ang Chita greeted us with relief and the glint of her gold-toothed smile. She brought flasks of tea to our grubby wooden table.

"Is your village okay?" she asked, innocently oblivious to how our worlds could not have been further apart. Her teahouse, like most, was almost deserted. Small cracks had crawled up the wall, and she would not allow us to sleep in certain rooms she deemed unsafe. Her neighbour had drawn the short straw. The roof was drooping inwards, hanging by a thread and supported only by the corners of stone walls. One push would probably have finished it off. Even worse, this was where Pasang Temba had lived. His wife, children, and grandchildren were now living in a tent in the garden. For the first time, my sadness turned to anger. I could only ask "why?" at this needless destruction and waste. Innocent people had been dealt the cruelest hand of all, and for what, I did not know. That was the reality of life, and at times like these, it was hard not to hate it.

We arrived at Tengboche Monastery the next morning, which was far from the crumbly mess the rumours in the valley had foretold. The journey down to Lukla became more of an *Indiana Jones* tribute minus the bravado, as we legged it across suspension bridges and glanced around, fearful of landslides. The United States Geological Survey (USGS) predicted another large tremor, and I felt it was far from over, as did Tashi and Lakpa at Kyangjuma, who were sleeping outside under a tarpaulin in fear of the forthcoming aftershock. Tashi rushed out to hug us and brought us cheese toasties and biscuits from her bakery. Ama Dablam Lodge had survived the quake with little more than cracked bricks, and staying with them was the first thing I'd been able to look forward to—seeing familiar faces in a place that was otherwise disfigured.

That night, our team and the local monks were crowded around a miniscule TV with trays of popcorn. One of the monks came over to ask us if we had an iPhone charger. This was the most surreal situation I had ever been in. Somehow, they had a connection to CNN News, and we got our first glimpse of the chaos we were heading into. When I'd learned about earthquakes at school I had imagined flattened homes and devastation. As we edged closer to the epicentre, I saw I had been right. Entire villages were reduced to scrap heaps with people buried beneath. There were injuries and suffering like I had never seen, and the international aid effort was already in full force. It sounded as bad as it looked. We saw scenes of the destroyed landmarks we loved and heard reports of the rising death toll.

The news also reported that the Ministry of Tourism had declared the mountain still open, which explained the passing porters carrying ladders up the trail with SPCC (Sagarmatha Pollution Control Committee) marked on the side—the organisation responsible for fixing the route through the Khumbu Icefall. I assumed that pretending the route was open was another ploy to invalidate our permits. Either way, I wouldn't be turning around. They were wasting time and resources on a mountain that almost everyone had left, instead of focusing on the relief effort. It only added to my frustration. Sadly, the media focused on the area where just a few hundred foreign citizens had been endangered, and that happened to be Everest, whilst hundreds of thousands of Nepali people had lost everything.

To their credit, the Nepalese were always generous. Before we trekked down the next day, Tashi hurried over to hand me something: an elegant, handcrafted purse with a bracelet inside.

"You give this to your girlfriend!" she beamed. I laughed and said I didn't have one, but when Tashi insisted, nobody bothered trying to resist. It didn't feel right to take anything—we were not the victims—but such a beautiful gesture was a light in the otherwise bleak situation.

I braced myself to discover more on the weak internet signal provided by the Everest Bakery in Namche Bazaar, which had fared considerably better than everywhere else. I found the response back home had been astronomical. It hadn't occurred to me until then just how many people were worried and rooting for me. When the media weren't dragging us away for interviews, our heads were buried in touch screens all afternoon. I tried to scour the news articles and make sense of it all. Dad had registered me with the Foreign Office to try and get me home, and I saw my name plastered on several articles. I had been described as "safe" at Camp One, which was a little farfetched. Reading the confused reports made me impatient to get the facts straight. Closer to home, my own PR team consisting of Jenny Fives, Ste, and Chris, were working together to monitor my emails and social media channels.

At a glance, I wrongly assumed otherwise—I lost my temper and Chris had the misfortune of being in the firing range. Maybe I was so used to being in control. But I hadn't realised just how well they had managed the crisis, working around the clock answering over two hundred media enquiries and issuing press statements on my behalf, despite the crippled NCell network and my refusal to give live phone interviews. Jenny even had staff at the Westgrove office helping her sift through it all.

Whilst being worried sick themselves, they had kept me and my family safe from the journalists, who were so determined to secure a statement that they were banging on our front door. They probably would have interviewed Hector the dog had he been available for comment. I felt awful for putting them through all of this for my own dream, but I was absolutely delighted that my fundraising total for Nepal had almost tripled in the space of a few days.

Because of their updates, my presence in Nepal made a difference. Support for the Himalayan Trust was more important than ever. The media storm back home was the perfect opportunity to get people to respond to the disaster in Nepal by donating to rebuild the ruined country. When I finally had a chance to write a blog post about what happened, I spent hours on a bench reliving events I didn't particularly want to remember.

The connection to the outside world came at an even higher cost. One concerned person contacted me on Twitter to ask about one of her relatives at base camp. My heart sank when I learnt she had died just metres away from our camp. I couldn't find the words to respond. It could have been my own family in a desperate quest for answers, and only chance had decided otherwise. Usually I understood that life was luck of the draw, but now it had never felt so repugnant to be alive.

As I descended the forested hillside to Monjo, I couldn't help but notice how both extremes of Nepal—the stunning beauty and the abject poverty—still met in the same place. The enchanting greenery had survived. I stopped to drink beside the trail as a tiny Firecrest went about its day. It chirped sweetly and fluttered around a young fir tree, pecking at insects and fresh buds, before turning to acknowledge me, the pale-faced teenager stinking of cheesy crisps. Such a beautiful sight gave some sort of hope, a sign that life must go on. Dreams could be replaced, though lives could not.

CHAPTER 38

Dead Memories

"We all die. The goal isn't to live forever, the goal is to create something that will."—Chuck Palahniuk

In the thirty-eight mile span from base camp, the devastation had worsened two-fold, but Lukla had remained intact to hold the thousands trying to escape from the flimsy excuse of an airport terminal into Kathmandu. I was glad to see our trekking guide Dep Kumar with his usual cheer. His family was safe and despite his house being wrecked, he still managed his favourite catchphrase, "No worries, chicken curry!" Harnessing strength from my team distracted me and lifted my mood.

"Where are you from?" growled a bad-tempered security officer at the airport.

"Japan!" Rolfe said in his usual humour.

Even at Camp One, Rolfe had joked whether the Wi-Fi was working. Ingo, his usual unflappable self, had strolled around the tents cracking jokes in his blinding pants. Rob went beyond his responsibilities to look after others like me, getting us off the mountain, and applying his medical expertise without hesitation. He was a hero in my eyes.

Military helicopters and jets were lined up as we finally arrived at Kathmandu Tribhuvan Airport. Our taxi weaved through the city in a strange feeling of calm. Eight days after the earthquake, nobody seemed in a rush to get out anymore. Perhaps the locals had sprung to action before the dust had a chance to settle, because spotting the twisted wreckage of fallen buildings and infrastructure was more difficult than the fuzzy TV had suggested. A few buildings had slid off their foundations and bitten the dust, but the rescuers had long gone elsewhere. The humming tourist district of Thamel was mostly the same, and an untrained eye would have seen nothing untoward but the subdued atmosphere that had replaced the usual bustle of the streets. The residents were hushed, few smiled, and most kept their heads low.

Most of the modern buildings in the Kathmandu valley were robust enough to survive catastrophe, but many who worked in the centre of Kathmandu and lived in surrounding neighbourhoods faced an entirely different prospect. Our waiter told us his house was "finished" before carrying on serving us like any other day. Most people in the world would flap at the slightest inconvenience, like camping in the rain, but the Nepalese faced a monsoon season under nothing but canvas and seemed to brush it aside. They put on a brave face and tourists enjoyed the city as if nothing had happened.

I ate a few mouthfuls before my heart fluttered and jolted me up. My head pressed the panic button. My arms locked. I knew this loss of control well enough to rush to the restaurant bathroom and sit on the urine-stained concrete, waiting for the whirring vision to pass. Just like the tremor, my first panic attack in two years had come unannounced, when I thought it was in the past. It was over as quickly as it started, but I'd already hurried back to Hotel Manaslu with sweat pouring down my face to throw up.

I did not want to be there, lying in bed. I didn't want to be anywhere. BBC News wanted an interview, and friends and even strangers were inundating me with reassuring messages, but the world still felt empty around me. I spent the afternoon browsing the internet until another bout of dizziness startled me. The light dangling from the ceiling was swinging like a pendulum; the building was rocking. The shutters on the windows rattled, and the shuddering of the bed upset my stomach even more.

"Oh, just kill me already! Give it your best shot!" I spat aloud in anger, not bothering to move. The tectonic plates had destroyed enough lives around me that it only seemed fair to bring me down with everyone else. Downstairs, Aeneas described the way the screaming French relief doctors had darted into the courtyard as the windows of the hotel lobby flexed like wobble boards, until the valley floor fell still again after a few seconds.

I took a sight-seeing trip by taxi that I hoped would bring me some sort of closure. Driving down the road was like walking onto a movie set. I got out to see Dharahara, a nine-storey tower popular with families and tourists. It had snapped like a matchstick. A Nepalese soldier stood guard in silence. 180 bodies had been pulled from the rubble. Thinking of their last moments made me think I'd seen enough, but this was an opportunity to see things that I would hopefully never see again. The palaces, courtyards, and temples of the Kathmandu Durbar Square were a disheartening sight, with the ancient pagodas brought to the ground. Locals lay under makeshift shelters of tarpaulin in the middle of the square. At least two million people were already homeless in Nepal, and many others were the same because of the aftershocks that might bring their homes to the ground for good. Scorched sports fields and golf courses were decorated with the tents of hundreds of people seeking refuge. I wondered if Nepal would ever be the same again.

I haggled the taxi driver down in price, then realised my cruelty and handed him extra. What I had seen in forty minutes was bad enough, and central Kathmandu had fared better than the surrounding districts where the most desperate humanitarian crisis was still in full swing. Sindhupalchowk district had suffered a much higher fatality rate, whilst to the east and the epicentre of the quake, Gorkha had suffered fewer casualties, but homes were destroyed and the farming villages flattened, the livestock putrefying beneath. Locals didn't bother to look at the helicopters overhead. Aid was focused on the capital and they were all but forgotten.

I knew their resourcefulness could only go so far, and I considered joining the few climbers who decided to stay and join the relief effort. Search teams, Nepali soldiers, and foreign aid workers were assembling from across the globe to deal with the thousands of injured. But I was not an aid worker. I was not qualified, skilled, or medically trained. I was a handyman at best. The general consensus was that I should go home and ease the demand on resources. I had a family to consider, too.

I was looking for ways to help in the meantime. The Himalayan Guides office was mournful as I delivered an envelope of cash for the families of their staff. My newfound friend in Gokyo, another Tenzing, then Facebook messaged me from the middle of the Himalayas on their satellite internet. His mother had been seriously injured; he worried for her and their home in Khunde, now reduced to grey bric-a-brac. I transferred everything I could afford from my bank account. It wasn't much in my terms, but their gratitude made it feel like a million dollars. Letting them know they were not alone was the best consolation I could give them, and it made me feel better, too.

I had shrugged off the panic attack as a one-off, and it wouldn't stop me from touring around the city with Aeneas for two days before I left. We shook hands and I left to catch my flight. That was it. Aeneas had been great company. He probably felt otherwise, considering my filthy sleeping bag at Camp One; the piss-taking had continued long down the valley. We should have been summit buddies, but now the only thing we could celebrate was life.

Sure enough, once this support network was gone, I hit the bottom. I had little fight left in me. Reading about the British trekker who'd been killed in the avalanche that buried the village of Langtang made me feel sick. The Doha Airport was the last place I expected to be huddled up in the corner fighting tears.

I had long believed adversity was the greatest teacher, but I learnt that nothing teaches you more about life than death. I could never again underestimate the brutality of nature, and the harrowing consequences would follow me forever.

CHAPTER 39

Homecomings

"Coming back to where you started is not the same as never leaving." —*Terry Pratchett*

6th MAY 2015

Once home, the horror show spit me back out into reality. The polished terminal of Manchester Airport was alienating. I had never been so afraid, or embarrassed, to see my own family. Before the Arrivals lounge, I hesitated, fearing a huge crowd to greet me on the other side. I counted to three, lowered my head, and told myself it was all over now. Mum and my stepdad were happier to see me than I was them. I couldn't bear to look at either.

"I'm fine," was all I could say. Mum didn't listen as she squeezed the air from my chest. I was already looking for the door.

As we pulled into our driveway I saw the delicate pink blossoms on our apple tree; I was somewhere I might feel safe again. The grass was green and the air was warm, if only for a little while. Only when I smelled the rotting expedition clothing inside my kitbag could I truly appreciate home. I scooped Hector up in my arms and his tail wagged like it had in the video.

He's not the Messiah, he's a very naughty boy!

Before I could adapt to normal, like safe drinking water and stable tectonic plates, a taxi whisked me away to the ITV studios at Media City in Manchester. The driver complimented me on how beautiful my village was, something I had always taken for granted. It was a blessing just to stand and listen to the birds chirping away, like the Firecrest I had watched in the Khumbu.

I was asked in all of my interviews if I would make a third attempt on Everest. As far as I could see, there was no "third time lucky"—creating your own luck doesn't apply on Everest, and if it did, what had the people killed at base camp done that was so wrong? The Everest poster on my wall was banished to my cupboard, but the mountain was everywhere I looked, even in the newspapers collecting on our table. It was safe to say my sponsors had not fallen short on mainstream media coverage despite my not reaching the summit. I had prepared myself to be discarded like an outdated advert once again, but I was wrong. Maybe my dreams couldn't be replaced so easily after all, especially one that had taken every ounce of my conviction and grit.

My homecoming dinner of spaghetti Bolognese, whilst a pleasant change from egg fried rice, left a bitter taste in my mouth. All I could think about were the Sherpas and their families who would never eat together again. I wished the avalanche had taken me instead of them. I played out scenarios of what else could have happened, like finding my teammates buried, or being injured myself. I wasn't waking up screaming in the middle of the night, but it will live with me for the rest of my life. Even our journalist companion Tom, after being shot at and nearly blown up in Afghanistan, declared that Camp One was the closest he'd come to accepting he was going to die. His BBC documentary on the disaster gave me a few sleepless nights, but that was nothing compared to the worries keeping the Nepalese people awake under their flimsy tarpaulin shelters in monsoon rains. After watching the documentary, my grandma left me a voicemail saying how proud she was as she choked back tears.

It seemed everyone was simply glad to have me home, but when so many others weren't returning, I had no reason to smile. Everyone seemed to want a piece of me over the coming days. Even walking through my village felt like I was being pointed at. I didn't know how to feel, so I ignored the lot, until the doorbell rang and I reluctantly answered. I was met with a smile from one of my kitchen colleagues, Dan, with his cheerful Lancashire accent and easy-go-lucky outlook. He had called by to reassure me, and I appreciated knowing that people supported me for the person I was rather than what I did. At the time, though, his support fell on deaf ears.

Mum was especially worried about me and badgered me to speak to people. It was unlike me to push my friends and mentors away. The only exception was my teammate Dr. Rob Casserley, who called a few days later. He was one of few who had been through the same experience—one that people at home could not understand. Mum said I could throw it all away. I felt I already had.

I eventually went into a rage and shouted, threw things, and thrashed around the kitchen. Fearing I would lash out at others too, I hid in solitude for almost a week and passed the time on whatever I could motivate myself to do. It seemed like there was no point in trying to evade the depression like I usually did. At least I was strong enough to stop it from getting any worse. My goal-centric driving force had been extinguished by the goal itself, and I felt guilty for not doing anything about the problem, because I wasn't sure what I could do. My passion was inspiring people to overcome adversity by overcoming my own. What if I let mine win? My mind was troubled. I wasn't ready to slam shut the brightest chapter on my life, but I saw no alternative other than to give into my fear of living an average existence.

One friend, Rich Whitehouse, persevered in calling me until I finally answered. Rich knew the near-death experience far better than me. Back in the early nineties when he was not much older than me, he had seen innocent citizens gunned down in Bosnia whilst serving as a Royal Engineer in the British Army. The year earlier he won a bravery award for chasing down an arsonist barefoot in the middle of the night and breaking his wrists before handing him over to the police. He was the sort of guy I didn't have the balls to ignore for too long.

There was not an ounce of empathy in his voice. He was ruthless and to the point.

"Have you killed the people at base camp? No. So why are you mourning them?" he began.

"It could have been me," I said weakly.

"But it wasn't. And they wouldn't give a shit about you if it was," he barked back. I could barely speak. But we learn the most by simply listening, not talking.

"You have to use this as an opportunity to grow. Everest served its purpose. It's given you something regardless of whether it was what you wanted. And it's probably the best thing that could ever happen to you. Grow from it."

"How?" I gulped, but Rich's words enforced what I already knew. The determination he had seen inside of me six months earlier during the Three Peaks Cycle Challenge was still inside. It just needed a way out.

I still remember the way his words turned my situation around. Feeling bad in such circumstances wasn't really a choice—but choosing not to stand up and fight was. That phone call was just what the doctor ordered, as the next day I resurfaced with the passion I feared I had lost.

I quickly signed myself up to climb Aconcagua in Argentina, the highest peak in South America, with my Everest teammate Rolfe Oostra. Aconcagua was a challenging yet achievable objective to satisfy my fix for extreme challenge without breaking the bank. The thought of adventures around the world and breaking world records danced the tango in my head. I was buzzing.

I also discovered a phenomenon called "Everesting," which entailed cycling the same distance as the height of the mountain in less than twenty-four hours. It was a chance to win, both metaphorically and physically. I committed myself straight away. If I couldn't climb Everest the standard way, I would climb it on my bike.

I accepted that I would never know why I was spared on the mountain when so many others were not, but no amount of procrastinating could bring them back. At nineteen and with my life ahead of me, I couldn't let it ruin me, because in my heart I owed it to Pasang Temba, Kumar, Tenzing, and everyone at base camp to pursue my dreams and help the victims rebuild their lives. That way, when my time came, I would have an epitaph to be proud of. People told me that I'd already achieved enough, but I would never settle for anything less.

I finally went for a coffee with Chris Spray. If there was ever a time for a man-hug, this was it. He let me do the talking.

"So, what's next?" he asked. When I said that I wasn't sure I wanted to climb Everest anymore, he simply interjected, "at the moment..."

Although I first thought he was being negative, he had a point. I didn't need Everest at the moment. For the first time in my life, I didn't feel the rush or obligation. I hadn't quit. Everest was merely a stop on my journey.

CHAPTER 40

Falling off the Wagon

"Sometimes, not getting what we want is a wonderful stroke of luck."—Dalai Lama

By now, I knew that the route to success was about as robust as the rickety ladders that bridged the chasms of the Khumbu Icefall. There was no excuse for not trying. Rediscovering myself was far from straightforward, but I was ready to face the challenge. Bouncing back was what I did best.

There was no time to waste, and Steve Fives had eagerly wanted to see me. I sat down on an elegant sofa on their patio and glanced around, unsure what to say at first. Most people didn't know what to say to me, either. Foremost, Steve and Jenny wanted to know I was okay. I wasn't just okay; I was back and ready to fight.

I had already begun to babble away about my Aconcagua expedition and new plans. Steve listened with a relieved smile, delighted I was refusing to surrender my passion. He knew me well enough to expect nothing less. I nearly spat out my coffee when he revealed that the Westgrove board had already decided to continue my Young Ambassador role. They were with me for the journey, not just the summit, as he had always told me. I now had a stream of financial support to bring my plans to fruition, and thankfully, leave the kitchen jobs behind. Westgrove would be with me for whichever adventure I chose. Right then, I felt like the luckiest adventurer in the world.

The team at Active Cheshire was equally warm and enthusiastic. Everyone crowded around me in the office. Anne rushed out of an important meeting to hug me. Despite our professional connection, she was often like a second mum. The staff were blown away by my new plans and spellbound by my stories. Speaking about the events in person helped me deal with them, too.

I received a phone call from a youth hostel in Windermere offering me a job as a team member. It sounded too good an opportunity to miss. Living in the Lake District, my second home, would give me some space to write my book, too; Wordsworth had lived there for a reason. Moving away from home so soon may not have been the smartest move, but settling in would just take a different kind of acclimatisation.

The historic hostel was tucked away on a country lane near Troutbeck Bridge. The building sat at the edge of the forest and faced Lake Windermere, the skyline of the Langdale valley mirrored in the water. On summer evenings I cycled down country lanes to picturesque villages and along the shoreline of Ullswater, smooth as glass. I felt so lucky to be there. The fresh Lakeland air blew the thoughts of the avalanche away, and sunrise at the jetty was the perfect place to sit and write undisturbed.

From the hostel I could go straight over to the Kirkstone Pass, the Lake District's highest pass open to traffic, where I trained for my Everesting attempt. The challenge channeled my energy into something positive, but was certainly a worry. Fewer than a hundred riders over the world had done it. As I pleaded with businesses to sponsor each ascent, one man urged me to reconsider, suggesting I would have only a fifty-fifty chance of survival. How ironic that would be, if I kicked the bucket trying to cycle up Everest instead. I'd heard it before, though. My body was well conditioned for such a feat. By this point, I'd received over one thousand pounds pledged for Nepal, so there was no backing out.

I was swamped again when I agreed to organise a fundraising walk for Nepal. When the day came, the fact that the local community cared enough to come for a walk in the pouring rain epitomised everything good about our society. Adventurer Squash Falconer was even cycling around the country to deliver chunks of Toblerone chocolate to anyone who donated to my charity donation page. I certainly wasn't short on support, but I was getting tired.

Normally I allowed my body some recovery after an expedition, but I had forgotten I was not invincible, and I paid the price. I came down with a virus that lasted for six weeks and made me wheeze until my ribs were tender to the touch. Split shifts meant I was rushing straight out to cycle ten ascents of the pass after work, while on the job I barely had the strength to carry linens up the stairs of the hostel. Afterwards I retreated to the farmer's field and caravan that I had found to stay in, where there were warped chipboard shelves taped to the wall, a hole in the rotten door frame, and no running water or sanitation. My post-expedition plan to relax and write my book had fallen a little flat—as I imagined the caravan might when heavy winds swept in from across the lake.

As the weeks slipped away, I began to hate the three-hour train journeys, eating from vending machines, and living out of a suitcase. Without the promise of Everest on the horizon, everything was becoming a struggle.

The Westgrove boardroom was packed for my first post-expedition talk. You could literally hear a pin drop, but not just from the horror of the story. I always knew when my stammer was having a bad day, and the story dragged out into a painful crawl of blocks and embarrassing pauses that I could not control. I even had to sit down at one point. The team showered me with positive feedback about my courage, but my confidence was in tatters. The Alex who left for Everest was different from the Alex who came back, but I was disappointed to learn the stammer had come back, too.

Every performer has bad days, but I had even more disasters over the coming weeks when my speech seized up completely. Desperation led me to try hypnotherapy, and despite being put into a trance, the only thing that vanished was hundreds of pounds from my wallet.

Exhaustion quelled my creativity, too. I could no longer strain at my laptop through bloodshot eyes at 1:00 a.m. I was making little headway on my book due to tiredness and my surroundings. Now I had to decide whether the benefits of training up in the Lakes outweighed the negatives. I quickly realised this was the wakeup call I needed to learn self-preservation. If I didn't do something, I risked becoming a one-hit-wonder like John Thomson had warned.

After deliberation, I handed in my notice. Leaving the hostel was a tough decision, but the right one. Besides the money, the job had been a blessing in disguise. Working at the hostel gave me a place to gather my thoughts, get back on my feet, work with great people, and reach my all-time peak fitness: most notably a resting heart rate of forty beats per minute.

I made it back in time to give a keynote presentation for young footballers at a prestigious conference centre. This was my last chance to reinstate my speaking confidence, and being in front of my own age group was never easy to begin with. I had prepared meticulously, and I stood up with every bit of conviction and passion I had left. The first few lines came as a fragmented mumble. "Not again," I thought.

You could have sliced the air with a knife as two hundred people waited for me to say something. A few puzzled faces caught the panic in my eyes. Then, right on cue, the hairs stood up on my arms, and I imagined Kumar beaming at me in the front row. He smiled at me, and I smiled back. My heart took over and I commanded the huge room. I could feel the audience hanging on my words right until the very end of an applause that carried on long after I had sat down. I could feel on top of the world without actually being there.

The feedback was overwhelming—some people even told me that it had changed their life, and weeks later, a grateful father thanked me because his epileptic daughter came home beaming with confidence after I spoke at her college. That was the only reason I needed to carry on. To think I had been moments away from clicking my finger to send a sick note, fearing I couldn't deliver, was most frightening of all.

We all have to make money, but I would take the money I needed to survive rather than working to take everything I could. Either way, I had to keep planning challenges if I was to make a living from telling my story and get paid for the person I had become. If I quit telling the story, how could I inspire people? This was the life I'd chosen, and if I kept the compass pointing in the right direction, I would live it to the fullest. I just had to keep going, and remember why I started.

CHAPTER 41

Adapt and Overcome

"Things work out best for those who make the best of how things work out."—John Wooden

On 6th August 2015, at 2:15 a.m., I climbed Mount Everest. On my bike.

127 miles and twenty-one hours later, 29,304 feet of vertical ascent was in the bag. Nobody was there to hear me shouting "Summit!" over the buffeting Pennine helm winds, but I didn't care. After fourteen consecutive ascents of up to twenty-five percent gradients, standing atop Great Dun Fell in Cumbria alone in the darkness was little more than an inconvenience.

As I staggered around on the remote country lane opposite the local Christian centre, I could well have been knocking on heaven's door, if not for Ste ushering me to the safety of Mick's car. He knew I would not stop. An unsuccessful bid to climb Everest on my bike would have crushed me. As always, Ste stepped out of the limelight as I took the credit. He was probably as glad to see the back of it as I was.

With so many positive people around me, I didn't need the negative anymore. Having people around me to share my vision was more of a gift than the destination. Even without the summit, I had finally gained something I had always wanted: my own approval. That was what I needed to finally be happy. When I look back on it, reaching the summit on my first attempt and feeling satisfied with the achievement would have felt a little shallow. But of course, I still aim for the top, for the same reason there are footsteps on the moon. If you boarded a plane to Monaco and ended up in Milton Keynes, you'd be a little miffed—although, you could always jump on a bike and cycle the rest. Just don't ask me for directions.

My Everest 2015 project also raised over 20,500 pounds for charity—more than half for the Nepalese earthquake victims, and the rest for adversity in Cheshire, in particular to support a disabled gymnast's training costs to reach her potential and use her story to inspire others. That alone made everything worthwhile for me. However, whilst raising money helps us leave the world better than how we found it, there is no shortage of people doing challenges for causes close to their heart, and long may that continue.

I'm no Bob Geldof, but I believe the biggest potential for change lies in the mindset of other people, because until we change our minds, we cannot change a thing. Overcoming my adversity, however insignificant to some, continues to inspire others in whatever circumstances they may face. Perhaps it's overcoming an impairment, getting out of bed and fighting depression, or choosing not to believe the lies that bullies tell. If reading my story encourages just one person to raise their middle finger at their own adversity, then the multiplier effect continues, and I have succeeded. As far as inspiring others to get more physically active, well, having the word "Everest" printed on the back of my cycling vest is enough to tempt some to race past me, maybe to boost their ego a little. I always watch on in amusement. I've accepted that I will forever be a bean pole, and, fortunately, I don't need to be fast to climb Everest.

Each of us have to climb our own Everest, be it in the everyday or on the highest peak in the world. Both are an uphill battle through the Icefall, which in my vivid experience, can trigger an avalanche at any moment. All we can do is nurture our dreams. Sometimes these difficult experiences change us before we have the chance to learn from them. That was true in my case, but even if my goal was too big, I have since grown into the person who will achieve it when the opportunity comes. I often forget I'm only twenty years old, though as I have written, age knows no boundaries to the lessons I've learned. What I am still learning is that life owes us nothing more than life itself, and anyone who believes otherwise becomes their own biggest obstacle.

Back in the comfort of home—my happy place—I often take a minute to gaze at the quote on my wall, still inscribed in pen: "The greatest suffering brings the greatest successes." Playing it safe might not have hurt anyone, but it wouldn't have inspired many, either. In my eyes, dreaming is better than doubting, and doing is better than dreaming.

Don't get me wrong, I'm no thrill seeker. And that's fine. Not knowing exactly where my journey will leave me is the biggest thrill of all, because whatever happens next will be fate, which I cannot control. It's how I handle the consequences that will determine the rest. By now, I know I have everything I need.

This is who I am, and this is my journey so far. Like everyone, I have my challenges—but they sure don't have me.

EPILOGUE

I t was a Friday morning like any other. I'd had a lazy autumn spin around the Cheshire plain. However long I tried to prove otherwise, I think everyone needs some fun sooner or later. I was finally able to enjoy the outdoors and the mountains for what they were once I let go of the pressure.

It's nice to have things working in my favour sometimes, but I don't want to be too far from a problem to deal with—it only makes me suspicious—and those routine sixty mile rides also gave me plenty of time to work out how I might overcome the next challenge.

After a hasty shower I hurried downstairs in smarter attire. I downed my coffee, grabbed my laptop, and headed for the door to an expedition meeting.

"Be careful," Mum called out as usual.

"See you later," I replied, rolling my eyes a little.

I paused in the hallway. There was no better time than the present.

"Oh... by the way, Mum?" I began. She put the kettle down and looked over at me intently. I took a deep breath.

"...You do know I'll have to go back, don't you?"

ACKNOWLEDGEMENTS

Life has mysterious ways, but everything seems to happen for a reason. Sometimes it takes a long time, perhaps a lifetime, to discover the reason something has happened, and other times we may simply never know. When I put my boots on and set off on my journey to climb Mount Everest, it didn't really matter what I knew—but who I had around me. The influence of the people you meet on such a long and winding road will always be present, even when the dream changes direction and hangs in the balance, and the boots are battered beyond recognition. I will be forever grateful for the best support team I could have asked for. Thank you for believing in me when I often didn't believe in myself and picking me up when I was down on my knees, even if I didn't deserve it.

Although I may have loosened a few screws during my exploits, the list that follows is not exhaustive, so please forgive me for simply lacking the space to acknowledge everyone who has helped me. We do not succeed on our own. We grow and learn together. And we're going to have one hell of a party some day.

Foremost, thanks to my mum, Debbie, for being my rock, giving me the best in life, understanding my passion, and supporting everything I do, however much it scares her. Thank you to my stepdad, Chris, for looking after Mum and holding down the fort when my exploits were giving her kittens.

Thanks to my dad, Pete, for teaching me more about life than I have often given him credit for, and for helping me discover the world of adventure and fitness that have brought me to where I am today. To both of my grandmas, I apologise for giving you wrinkles prematurely. To the rest of my extended family, thanks for a loving childhood. To my dogs, Harley and Hooch, thanks for being the best friends I could ever ask for and showing me how simple and fun life can be.

High on this list is my mentor, Chris Spray, for teaching me an immeasurable amount about myself and the capabilities I never knew I had, and for never once giving up on me or my dream. And thanks to his wife, Bethany, for tolerating the undying commitment and time he gave to nurture my growth to maturity. Having someone to ask, "What's next?" got me right where I needed to be.

Thanks also to one of my closest friends, Ste Rumbelow, for always being by my side as a confidant and all-around guru who I can count on for anything, whatever the hour of day, without expecting anything in return. It was thanks to Everest that we met, and I'm glad we did.

I'm extremely grateful to Steve Fives at The Westgrove Group for his dedicated mentoring and genuine belief in my journey that elevated me to a whole new level of my adventure career and made the EPIC7 mission possible. I look forward to what we can achieve next. And to his wife, Jenny, for keeping me organised—no mean feat—and pulling the media crisis together after the avalanche.

I owe thanks to Brigadier John Thomson OBE QVRM TD MSC RCDS for his time spent coaching a nervous stammering teenager and turning him into a successful adventurer and professional speaker. Thank you for patiently guiding me through the numerous "grey zones" on my journey.

To my major sponsors in 2014, I'm sorry I couldn't literally take you to the top. To the directors and team at Textlocal Ltd., thanks for becoming the first major sponsor of my Baruntse and Everest expedition. Investing so heavily in my dream gave me the momentum and belief I needed to continue my journey through to the finish. And to Quintessential Finance Group, particularly Greg Cox and Mike Ransom, thank you for being the final piece of the puzzle for my boyhood dream and bringing my Everest 2014 expedition together at the very last minute. I will be forever thankful.

For 2015, I'm indebted to Anne Boyd and the whole team at Active Cheshire for their financial support and for sharing my passion to make a difference in the lives of others. As their Active Lifestyle Ambassador, I'm proud to be associated with the work they do—helping more people across Cheshire get more active, more often.

Thanks to all at The Westgrove Group, especially Steve and Jenny Fives, Simon, and Claire for becoming part of a compelling journey, and for embracing me into their community across the country as their first ever Young Ambassador. Entrusting me to inspire others to achieve their own Everest in life has already been a privilege.

I owe no less thanks to Camp Two sponsor Dennis Ryan, the team at Dayinsure.com in Tarporley, and Great Bear Distribution in Tattenhall, especially Carl Johnson. To all at the Chester Business Club and the alliance supporters, thank you for welcoming me into your club as a proud Young Ambassador—a role that has opened so many doors for my future. I am also honoured to be an ambassador for World Merit, a global platform of change makers. Thanks to Marj Boyer for the introduction. Together we really can make the world a better place.

I owe a huge thanks to Paul Daniels at thebestofchester for his networking that led to some amazing opportunities. To my expedition sponsors, a big thanks to Spencer and the guys at Cammell-Laird (third time lucky?), Mark Brocklehurst and David Griffiths at the Sharples Group, Fraser at Pescado Ltd., Andrew Donaldson at BiG Storage, Craghoppers UK (particularly Aidan and the sales team), Mark and Jamie Starr at Ideal 365 Workwear, Giles Warburton at Shortlist Recruitment, Nigel at LL Barrowcliff (and colleagues who supported my Baruntse trip), the Jeremy Willson Charitable Trust, Doug at Collingwood Recruitment, and Ralawise.

To my supporters, the Youth Hostel Association (YHA) and Scottish YHA, thanks for providing me with great accommodations during the EPIC7. Thanks to all at Marmot UK, Powertraveller, and LED Lenser for the equipment. I owe a special thanks to the reporters at the Chester Chronicle and Gavin at Chester Dee 106.3 who've continued to support me and my fundraising efforts over the years.

Thanks to Ian White and Mitch Smith at the University of Exeter for their patience and commitment to getting me in the best possible shape for my expeditions, especially when I took to weight lifting like a cat on water. Thanks also to the Mill Health Club in Chester and The Edge Cycleworks for keeping my steed in working order. One day I'll learn to fix a chain myself, I promise. Also thanks to Francis Blunt for helping me get essential training under my belt in 2014 when I was strapped for cash.

Thanks to all at Himalayan Guides, my expedition leader Tim Mosedale, Henry Todd, Kame Sherpa, Dr. Rob Casserley, Marie-Kristelle Ross, and my teammates both in 2014 and 2015 for making the best of two tragic and difficult situations.

There are so many individuals that have been pivotal pieces of my jigsaw in various ways. In particular, I'd like to thank Tom Crotty, Chris Pownell, Dan Hallett, Paul Robinson White, Jeff Smith, Lord Lieutenant of Cheshire David Briggs, Heidi at Forresters of Kingsley, Tim Kenney, Hems de Winter, Adrian Lomas, Stewart Kellett and the team at British Cycling, Simon Gerrard at the Cheshire FA, Gary Spinks, Giles Babbidge, Steve Platt, Andy Porter and the team at Veracity Digital, Guillaume at REACT (Red Endangered Animal Connection Trust), Mark Pinnock, Graham Wilkinson at Hampshire Flag Company, Tim Moss, Richard Whitehouse, Derek Jones at Kuoni UK, Russell Smith, Keiran Hewkin, and Steve at Sarah's Embroidery & Print. I also owe thanks to Becky Bellworthy, James Ketchell, Matthew Dieumegard-Thornton, Mollie Hughes, Bonita Norris, and Rhys Jones for inspiring me—I wish you the best of luck with your future adventures.

And a bit closer to home... thanks to Samantha Rogers for nominating me to carry the Olympic Flame—it changed my life. I'm extremely grateful to Craig and the Fifty Fingers band, Ian Thompson, Diane Mitchell and Harry Gilbertson, Sarah Lee and the Tarporley High Sixth Form staff, Pamela Zborowski, Nadia Fortune-Nesbit, John Holmes at APS Group, Paul Crewe at Smart Money, Rob Tudor, Geoff Dutton, Katherine Jackson, Tarvin Educational Foundation, Spinney Day Nursery, Vivio Chester, Dan Whitmore, John Hammond, Mike Gollings, and so many more in my local area for their continuous help with my fundraising efforts. Thank you to all who attended and supported my various fundraising events.

Two of my closest friends, Andy Bell and Barbara Wilkie, need a mention for their undying support, enthusiasm, and "Grumpy Cat" photos—they will know what I mean. I won't begin to list the rest of my friends, training companions, and those who I met on my adventures, but I will thank them for the great company. You know who you are.

I want to say hi to all of the Coca-Cola Future Flames—I didn't want to be selective, but I particularly wanted to thank Richard, Rachel, Christina, Kim, Anne, Holly, Katie Bennett, and Ron for their fundraising and moral support. Keep burning bright, Torchies.

And of course, I'd like to thank my adventure heroes. Bear Grylls, thanks for the inspiration and supporting my book. Thanks to Squash Falconer, Sir Ranulph Fiennes, Mark Wood, and Sir Chris Bonington OBE for encouraging me and kindly donating their time to support a young adventurer following in their footsteps.

INDEX

A

Abergwengregyn, 150
Abu Dhabi, 106
Acharya, Bhim, 130
Aconcagua, 239, 241
Active Cheshire, 166-167, 175, 177, 242, 252
Adventures Global team, 210
Aiguille du Midi, 156
Alpine Ascents International, 122
Alps, 33, 46, 48-49, 151, 157-158
Ama Dablam, 112, 117, 181, 183, 225-226
Ambleside, 159-160
Amphu Labsa Pass, 87, 150

Anxiety, 9, 11, 23, 39, 41, 59, 71, 92, 146, 172, 201
Arnette, Alan, 124
Ashby, Phil, 46
Asian Trekking, 214
Athlete, 6, 37, 39, 51-52, 65, 137
Atkinson, George, 54
Auxerre, 154
Aviemore, 98, 171
Axelsson, Ingolfur (Ingo), 125, 187-189, 230

B

Ballachulish Horseshoe, 173
Barclay, William, 3
Baruntse, 62, 64-65, 77, 80, 83-88, 91, 96, 99,

110, 116-117, 125, 150, 251, 253

BBC, 42, 44, 188, 231, 237

Beaumont, Mark, 159

Bellworthy, Becky, 34-35, 37, 58-59, 152, 254

Ben Nevis, 20-21, 23, 30, 97, 162, 176

Benegas, Damian, 205, 207

BiG Storage, 252

Binnean Beag, 170

Binnein Mor, 170

Biology, 9, 18

Black Ice, 13

Blencathra, 23

Blog/blogging, 17, 108, 122, 128, 138, 154, 177, 228

Blunt, Francis, 78, 80-86, 99, 150, 253

Bonington, Chris, 40, 61, 174, 254

Boot Inn, The, 34, 158

Borneo, 28, 144

Borrowdale, 160

Bosnia, 238

Boyd, Anne, 166-167, 177, 242, 252

Bradshaw, Jo, 187, 216-217

Brain condition, 9

Branson, Richard, 66

Briant, Nigel, 121

Brice, Russel, 111, 127-128

Briggs, David, 253

British Army, 100, 238

British Cycling, 167, 253

British Parliament, 17

Brown Slabs, 28

Brownsea Island, 94

Buddhist, 113, 117, 127

Bulkeley, Lucy Rivers, 121

Bully/bullying, 10, 22, 177

C

Cadair Idris, 98

Cairngorms National Park, 98

Calder, Tim, 127

Cammell-Laird, 252

Canary Wharf, 66

Cancer, 5, 28, 40, 45, 132, 138, 144, 163

Cardiff, 74, 91

Carlisle, 161

Casserley, Rob, 120-121, 125, 127, 187, 192, 197, 201-202, 206-207, 213, 230, 237, 253

Cessna 152 propeller plane, 78

Chamonix, 28, 46, 151, 154-157

Cheshire FA, 166, 253

Cheshire Wildlife Group, 17

Chester, 4, 35, 39-42, 50, 100, 140, 145, 151, 175, 252-254

Chester Business Club, 100, 145, 175, 252

Chester Chronicle, 35, 253

Chester Dee 106.3, 253

Chhiring, Lhakpa, 219, 221

China/Chinese, 5, 61, 145, 219

Cho Oyu, 115

Cholatse, 117

Chomolungma, 23, 131

Christmas, 12, 16, 36, 58, 96, 167-168

Chukhung village, 185

Chukkung Ri, 184

Churchill, Winston, 50, 64, 136

CNN, 226

Cobain, Kurt, 43

Coca Cola Future Flames, 254

Coe, Sebastian, 101

Coire an't-Sneachda, 171

Collingwood Recruitment, 253

Confucius, 34

Coniston, 149

Cool, Kenton, 117

Cox, Greg, 101-103, 252

Craghoppers UK, 68, 252

Crampons, 21, 192

Crampton, Phil, 127, 212

Craven, Philip, 175

Crawford, Roger, 8

Crib Goch, 150

Crotty, Tom, 253

Cumbria, 72, 246

D

Dahl Baht, 83, 110, 117, 218

Daniels, Paul, 100, 252

Dayinsure.com, 252

Delamere Forest, 35

Depression, 36, 51-52, 58, 145, 238, 247

Derwentwater, 160

Devaney, Paul, 214

Dharahara, 232

Diamox, 82, 206

Diana Award, 66

Dieppe, 153

Dieumegard-Thornton, Matthew, 35, 171, 254

Dingboche, 117

Divorce, 11

Dizzee Rascal, 39

Dom de Mischabel, 157

Domhutte, 157

Donaldson, Andrew, 252

Dorset, 94

Dr. Jayaram, 10

Dr. Seuss, 184

Drumnadrochit, 172

Dudh Kosi River, 109

Dughla, 186

Dumbarton, 161

E

Edge Cycleworks, 253

Edinburgh, 186

Einstein, Albert, 153

Ellis, Linda, 76

Elterwater, 176

Emerson, Ralph Waldo, 26

EPIC7, 149, 158, 168, 171, 173, 178, 180, 221, 251, 253

Epilepsy, 9-10, 28, 67, 90

Everest Bakery, 181, 227

Everest, George, 23

Exercise/exercising, 6, 27, 62, 94, 96

F

Facebook, 34-36, 39, 60, 122, 185, 233

Fe, Zhenfang, 219

Fethiye, 17

Fiacaill Ridge, 171

Fiennes, Ranulph, 61, 77, 150, 254

Firecrest, 229, 236

Fish & chips, 7

Fives, Jenny, 148, 177, 228, 241, 251-252

Fives, Steve, 145, 148, 166-167, 176-177, 241, 251-252

Foel Fras, 150

Fogle, Ben, 94

Foo Fighters, 20, 32, 52

Football, 6, 16, 53, 75, 120, 244

Forest, 5, 18, 20, 27, 32, 35, 46, 66, 68, 75, 80, 98, 152, 157, 165, 172, 197, 229, 242

Formula One, 61

Forrest Gump, 36

Forresters of Kingsley, 253

Fort Augustus, 172

Fort William, 20, 161, 169, 171, 173

Fotedar, Renu, 219

France, 7, 27, 156

Franklin, Benjamin, 191

Fred Whitton, 149

Fredinburg, Dan, 216

G

Gale, Dick, 189

Gandhi, Mahatma, 130

Garmin, 152, 159, 168

Germany, 163, 182

Gerrard, Simon, 166

Girawong, Marisa Eve, 219

Glacier, 46, 86, 120, 122-123, 186, 188, 192, 199, 201, 203, 207, 209-211, 217, 219

Glasgow, 161

Glen Nevis, 21, 97, 161, 170

Glencoe, 161

Glenmore Forest, 98

Global warming, 16

Glyder Fach, 150

Glyderau, 144

Gokyo, 116, 182, 233

Gorak Shep village, 124, 128, 188, 210

Gouter hut, 47

Great Dun Fell, 246

Great Glen Way, 171

Greece, 37

Grylls, Bear, 30, 53-54, 106, 122, 160, 254

Gyalgen, Dorje, 117, 127, 132

Gyan, 190, 198, 212, 222

H

Hampshire, 34, 253

Handbridge, 40

Handy, Chris, 113

Hardknott Pass, 149

Hazlitt, William, 224

Helicopter, 79, 82, 118-120, 130-131, 205-207, 209-210, 218-219, 221, 230, 233

Helmuth von Moltke the Elder, 88

Heraclitus, 178

Hermann Bakery, 184

High altitude cerebral edema, 82

Hillary, Edmund, 20, 108

Himalayan Guides, 120-121, 190, 211, 221, 233, 253

Himalayan Rescue Association (HRA), 214

Himalayan Trust UK, 144, 174, 181

Himalayas, 23, 62, 107, 137, 154, 170, 179, 233

Hinku Valley, 83

Hooch, 6, 32-33, 53, 68, 74-75, 99, 251

Horoshi, Yomagato, 219

Hospital, 5, 50, 64, 78, 81, 95

Hotel Manaslu, 106, 231

I

Ice axe, 21, 62, 219

Iceland, 125, 187

Ideal 365 Workwear, 252

Imja Khola valley, 117

International Mountain Guides, 120, 214

Isle of Anglesey, 6

Iswari, 118, 133

J

Jagged Globe, 125, 189, 216

James, Andy, 121

Japan, 219

Jeep, 18

Jeremy Willson Charitable Trust, 253

Jhyabu, 127, 190

Johnson, Brian, 151

Jones, Rhys, 58, 254

Jyoti, 181

K

Kala Patthar, 118, 124

Karate, 6, 14

Kathmandu, 78-79, 87, 106, 118, 120, 127, 134-

135, 179, 188, 212, 216, 218-219, 230-232

Kathmandu Tribhuvan Airport, 79, 230

Kellett, Stewart, 253

Kelsall, 4

Keswick, 28

Ketchell, James, 58, 99, 254

Khare village, 81

Khatri, Dorjee, 120

Khumbu Icefall, 119, 131, 193, 227, 241

Khumjung, 112

Khunde, 233

Kingston, Maxine Hong, 203

Kirkstone Pass, 99, 242

Kongma La, 118, 186

Kumar, Dep, 180, 230

Kyangjuma, 112, 133, 226

L

Lake District, 23, 28, 77, 98-99, 127, 149, 182, 242

Lakeland, 242

Lancashire, 237

Langdale, 242

Langtang, 233

Laxman, 108, 118, 191

Lee, Bruce, 142

Les Houches, 155

Letoonia Resort, 17

Levine, Alison, 138

Lho La, 194

Lhotse, 96, 116-117, 137, 183, 188, 209-210

Lingtren, 122, 211

Loch Linnhe, 173

Loch Lochy, 171

Loch Ness, 172

London, 27, 36-37, 39, 47, 57, 66, 73, 89, 121, 146, 151, 162, 187, 219

London Heathrow Airport, 47

Lukla, 79-80, 87, 108, 120, 133, 179, 219

M

Macclesfield headquarters, 101

Mackenzie, Scott, 121

Madison Mountaineering, 219-220

Mahalangur, 23

Maimonides, 174
Mallory, George, 105
Manang Air AS350 Eurocopter, 210
Manaslu, 91, 106, 231
Manchester, 5-6, 105, 170, 178, 235-236
Manchester Airport, 5, 105, 178, 235
Manchester United, 6
Mandela, Nelson, 94
Maralung, 114-115, 182
Marmaris, 17
Marmot UK, 253
Martienssen, Tom, 188
Matterhorn, 157
Media City, 236
Mera Peak, 81, 83-84, 108
Miliband, Ed, 162
Military, 53, 78, 96, 100, 189, 230
Mill Health Club, 253
Milroy, Oli, 94
Ministry of Tourism, 107, 125, 158, 227
Monastery, 113, 137, 189, 226
Monjo, 109, 229

Mont Blanc, 33-34, 45-46, 48, 50-51, 53, 74, 81, 138, 155-156
Monty Python, 130, 154
Mount Babadag, 18
MRI, 9, 50
Muir, John, 170
Mullach nan Coirean, 170
Mumbai Airport, 78, 88
Mungrisdale, 23

N

Namche Bazaar, 110, 180, 227
Neddermeyer, Dorothy, 13
Neuro-Linguistic Programming, 59
Newhaven, 152
NHS mental health department, 52
Nirvana, 117
Norris, Bonita, 58, 254

O

Obsessive-compulsive disorder, 11
Ogwen Valley, 173

Ogwyn, Joby, 122

Oldham, 5

Olu Deniz, 19

Olympic Torch Relay, 39

Ongchhu, 80, 82, 85

Onich, 62

Oostra, Rolfe, 187, 194,
    201-202, 217, 230, 239

Osteopath, 50

P

Palahniuk, Chuck, 230

Pangboche, 117, 120,
    133, 184, 212, 225

Panic attack, 9, 13, 16-
    17, 41, 72, 89, 99, 160,
    200, 231, 233, 244

Paraglide, 19, 35, 106

Pen yr Ole Wen, 150,
    173

Pescado Ltd., 252

Petite Fourche, 46

Pheriche, 224

Philippines, 39

Phortse village, 117, 183

Physiotherapist, 46, 62,
    95, 147

Podiatrist, 50

Poole Harbour, 94

Pownell, Chris, 253

Pratchett, Terry, 235

Puja blessing, 113, 126-
    127, 188-190, 213

Pumori, 119, 122, 191,
    208, 211

Q - R

Quintessential Finance
    Group, 101, 252

Rai, Krishna, 218

Ralawise, 253

Randa, 157

Ransom, Mike, 102, 252

Red Endangered Animal
    Connection Trust
    (REACT), 28, 45, 48-
    49, 144, 253

Red Wharf Bay, 7

Renjo La Pass, 116

River Dee, 41

Robbins, Tony, 44

Rockhopper mountain
    bike, 32

Romancini, Roman, 123,
    131, 134

Ross, Marie-Kristelle,
    120, 253

Royal Air Force, 188

Royal Oak, 22
Rugby, 10, 125
Ryan, Dennis, 252
Ryvoan Bothy, 98

S

Sagarmatha Pollution
  Control Committee
  (SPCC), 130-131, 220,
  227
Scafell Pike, 31, 160
Scotland, 20, 30, 37, 62,
  96-97, 161, 164, 168-
  169, 173, 199
Scottish YHA, 253
Sea Shepherd, 16
Seathwaite, 160
Seizure, 5, 9-10, 13, 52,
  67
Self-confidence, 8, 10,
  33, 41
Serac, 48, 119, 128, 199-
  200, 209
Sgurr a Mhaim, 169
Sharples Group, 252
Sheffield, 53, 78, 113
Sherpani, 114, 225
Shortlist Recruitment,
  252

Shrestha, Shiva Kumar,
  219
Shyakpa, 115
Simrik Air, 210
Sindhupalchowk, 232
Sirdar, 80, 120, 130, 188,
  190
Smith, Jeff, 91, 132, 253
Smith, Mitch, 95, 165,
  253
Snowdon Horseshoe,
  176
Snowdonia, 28, 98, 144,
  173, 176
Snowdonia National
  Park, 173
Solukhumbu, 79
Souther Fell, 23
Squash Falconer, 138,
  182, 243, 254
Stammer, 5, 14-15, 18,
  28, 37, 41, 59, 65, 101,
  147, 162, 174, 181, 243-
  244, 251
Steall Gorge, 170
Steck, Ueli, 107
Styhead Tarn, 160
Sweetland, Ben, 38
Switzerland, 157

T

Tabner, Reuben, 225

Tarporley, 10, 252, 254

Temba, Pasang, 117, 132,
190, 193, 205, 211-212,
218, 222, 226, 239

Temba, Phur, 80, 82-83,
182

Tengboche Monastery,
137, 226

Tenzing-Hillary Airport,
79

Tete Rousse Hut, 47

Textlocal Ltd., 71, 73,
146, 148, 251

Thacker, James, 157

Thain, James, 57

Thamel Eco Resort, 87

Thamserku, 117

Thoman, 80-81, 83

Thompson, Hunter, 217

Thomson, John, 100-
101, 103

Three Peaks Challenge,
28, 30-32, 34-35, 37

Thundu, Lhakpa, 190,
221

Thuraya satellite phone,
204

Tibet, 23

Todd, Henry, 122, 125,
127-128, 131-132, 185-
186, 202, 212-213, 218,
220, 253

Torchbearer, 36-37, 39-
40, 42-45, 50-51, 61,
144

Troutbeck Bridge, 242

Truong, Vinh B., 219

Tullet, Rachel, 214

Twain, Mark, 112

Tweddle, Beth, 40

Twitter, 69, 111, 122,
138, 228

U

Ullswater, 242

United States Geological
Survey (USGS), 226

University of Cumbria,
72

University of Exeter, 95,
253

V

Valin, Paul, 125

Valley of Silence, 194

Veracity Digital, 174, 253

Volunteer, 30, 39, 68, 147

W - Z

Waitley, Denis, 196
Wales, 6, 31, 150
Wallace, Daniel, 121, 190
Wallis, Jim, 124
Warrington, 145
West Cheshire Athletics Club, 36
West Highland Way, 171

Westgrove Group, 145, 148, 251-252
Whitehouse, Rich, 53, 161, 238-239, 253
Whittle, Simon, 148
Wildlife, 16-17, 26, 28, 45, 175
Wilkie, Barbara, 254
World Merit, 175, 252
Youth Hostel Association (YHA), 253
Zborowski, Pamela, 254

15798875R00151

Printed in Great Britain
by Amazon